Searching

Mary Moran

~~914 934~~ 1817

203. 531 7170

Searching

The Stories of Ireland's Missing People

Valerie Cox

BLACKWATER PRESS

Editor
Sinéad Lawton

Design & Layout
Melanie Gradtke

Cover Design
Melanie Gradtke

Additional Research
Emily Cox

ISBN
1-84131-634-2

Produced in Ireland by Blackwater Press, c/o Folens Publishers, Hibernian Industrial Estate, Greenhills Road, Tallaght, Dublin 24.

For my parents, Imelda and Des FitzPatrick, in Avoca, who have always given me their enthusiasm and their love.

Contents

Acknowledgements

This book came about after RTÉ producer Peter Woods suggested broadcasting a series of interviews on *Five Seven Live* with the families of missing people in Ireland. There was a huge reaction from listeners who wanted to help, to join in the search or to tell their own stories. John O'Connor of Blackwater Press then suggested expanding the initial six interviews and this book was born.

I would like to thank Emily Cox for her enthusiastic and persistent research work, and my journalistic colleagues, Elaine Keogh and Olivia Kelleher, who shared their own background material on missing people.

Thanks also to artist Frances Tyrrell, who held her own exhibition dedicated to the missing and who allowed me to reproduce her work. I am also grateful to Fr Aquinas Duffy, who founded and runs Ireland's Missing Persons website, for his help and guidance.

Thanks to my editor, Sinéad Lawton, who introduced me gently to the world of publishing, and to all the team at Blackwater Press.

Most importantly, thank you to all the families who allowed me into their lives and the lives of their missing loved ones.

I hope this book will prick the conscience of a man or woman who knows what happened to someone who has 'disappeared' or who knows where their body is hidden.

I hope you will read about the suffering of the families of those who have disappeared, who want to know what happened, who have no grave to visit.

You could put an end to their heartache. An anonymous phone call would do.

1

The Missing

Why Do They Disappear?

It's not like an illness, there are no symptoms, usually no indication that something is wrong and, for each missing person, there is a different reason for their disappearance.

It is important to distinguish between those who have chosen to disappear and those who are taken away, abducted or murdered. It is feared that many of the people listed as missing persons could be dead, but some of them may be out there reading this.

While some people do go missing in horrific circumstances, there are many other cases where the reasons are much less sinister, some people *choose* to disappear and there are many reasons why. Sometimes their marriage is in difficulty, sometimes things have gone even further and they may already have another family in another jurisdiction. One of the first people to draw attention to the double life lived by some of the Irish in the UK was Maeve Binchy. She wrote a play, *Deeply Regretted By*, about a man who had a family on both islands and the families only found out about it when the two 'wives' met at his funeral. These cases are fairly exceptional, but they do happen.

A man who was the foreman of a building site in England 15 years ago explained that a lot of 'missing people' from Ireland worked under him. It was an easy place to disappear. They would give their real identity to him to get a job but then live under a false name. Others would give him their identity cards and ask him to register them as employees and then disappear to South America or other places. They would have it worked out so that if people came looking for them, they would be thrown off the scent. At the time he didn't think anything of it. It was their business and indeed he was just helping them out.

Other people go away because they are in trouble. They may have been involved in crime, they may be pregnant, they may be trying to avoid an unpleasant situation. Often their families will know nothing of these things. For this reason, families are sometimes amazed when Gardaí investigate a disappearance and discover their loved one had led a somewhat secret life before they went missing.

Then there is acute disappointment, maybe with a job, an exam or a relationship. Some cannot face the deterioration of their social status, the lack of money or the fact that they may be made redundant. Some cannot admit to friends that they are unable to achieve academically. But, instead of sharing their fears with a friend or partner, they are too ashamed and leave home almost without realising what they are doing. If we could see into one another's souls then there is no doubt that we would help, that we would provide that listening ear and unconditional sympathy, but sometimes it is very hard to know, particularly when someone is learning to cover their tracks so well.

One thing that emerges time after time is that people don't plunder their savings accounts, take huge amounts of money away with them or organise savings in another jurisdiction. Often they don't even have a passport, yet we have heard of people turning up years later in places around the world where they would certainly have needed passports.

And we cannot ignore the fact that some people who leave may have close connections with the criminal underworld and may have accomplices organising everything for their departure.

There are also the young men who just walk away from home to follow an adventure someplace else. They may not intend to stay away so long without telling somebody, but the weeks drift into months and that reconnection becomes harder.

Some of these people don't consider themselves to be 'missing' at all. They drift around the world, make friends, start families and sometimes are quite annoyed to find themselves listed as 'missing'.

There was Kevin Crennan, whose story was reported by Olivia Kelleher in the *Irish Independent*. Dramatically, Kevin's family found out that he was alive after seven years without hearing a word from him. The 37-year-old was arrested in Colombia after he was found near an area controlled by the left-wing rebel group FARC. It was August 2001, shortly after the arrest of three Irishmen who have since been tried on charges of giving military support to FARC, and the Colombian authorities initially believed they had a fourth suspected IRA member.

Kevin's family were over the moon that he had turned up safe and well, but he was less enthusiastic. Fr Aquinas Duffy, who runs the Irish Missing Persons website, says 'I think Kevin was very annoyed about being classed as a missing person. Had he not been classed as missing, however, he would still be in jail. When he turned up, the Colombians thought he was an IRA man, but his family had him listed with Interpol.'

All the signs would have suggested he was never going to turn up. His passport had expired and his bank account was untouched.

Another person who didn't consider himself missing at all was James Patrick Byrne, a 33-year-old from Waterford. He had been living in Spain and had lost contact with his family for many years. They still hoped to get in touch however and, through Fr Aquinas' website, they pleaded with him to get in touch. James did make contact after a friend showed him the message.

It is important to remember that most missing people *do* turn up within a relatively short time frame. This book concentrates on the others, still missing after months or years.

Jumping to Conclusions

The experts tell us not to jump to conclusions when a car is found crashed into the sea or a pile of clothes is discovered neatly folded and abandoned on a beach. It's not necessarily a tragic accident or a drowning, it could be a decoy situation – maybe that is what the missing person wants people to think. Sometimes these people make contact with their families years later, after loved ones have lost all hope.

The important thing to remember is that for most people, leaving their home and family, a job, friends and even the family pets, takes enormous determination. Saying goodbye without letting anyone know that that is what you are doing is terribly hard and probably tells us a lot about the state of the mind of the individual concerned.

When the search gets underway, the family's plight is public knowledge and they may learn something they never knew about their loved one. It is very hard to read details of family spats, a mistress or an unplanned pregnancy in the newspapers, to see your loved one's face on television or posters in the street. It is very hard to be the one left behind and, in a sense, there is a form of grieving, without a body, without a grave to lay flowers on.

There is also the guilt, the guilt of wondering if you could have done things differently, if something you said was the catalyst to drive someone away. Most families finally have to concede that they were just living their normal lives with the narks and the rows and lack of time and the smiles and love and disappointment. In most cases, it is the person who is missing who has chosen another route and who didn't give them any notice.

It is generally accepted that the vast majority of those who are still on the missing list after many years have been abducted and murdered. In the following chapters you will read many stories of people who were there one moment and then suddenly… disappeared.

Some of the searches got underway almost immediately, in other cases there was a gap of several days before anyone realised that something unusual had happened. In some cases, the missing people were murdered almost at once, their killers never caught, never brought to justice.

Some of the families of the disappeared are convinced that they know the identity of their relative's murderer. In some small towns and villages people openly discuss the possibilities and name names. But the Gardaí cannot move in any of these cases because the people with hard information are refusing to come forward.

It is not a question of 'those who know' being 'those who did it' but, in a small community over many years, there had to be clues – the brother who came home covered in unexplained mud, the son who was digging in a remote corner of the farm, the late-night movements of a husband, a boat setting out to sea in bad weather, the disappearance of quantities of plastic sheeting, the unexplained shovel in the boot of the car. These are all things that the families of the disappeared believe other people must have seen. And what of the abductions themselves? People in small towns and even in cities notice a car slowing down to offer a lift to a young woman, or a young man being bundled into the back seat.

People hear rumours, about the new guy in town with a 'past', the hangers-on who have never actually done anything but who are thought to be unpleasant. And then there is the appalling scenario of the friend or family member who could be hiding a murderer, providing an alibi or simply turning a blind eye to what is happening around them. It is a fact that there are innocent people around us who are friends of murderers and who have a pretty good idea of what has happened to some of the people who disappeared. What is wrong with them? Are they afraid of retribution? Do they feel they will be in danger themselves? Are they content to live beside a man they know has violated and murdered a young woman? Are they not a little bit anxious that their own children could be in the hands of a man who they suspect has already killed?

And what of the missing bodies? What of Fiona Pender and her unborn baby? Jo Jo Dullard? Fiona Sinnott? The families of these women have accepted that their loved ones are dead but they cannot locate their bodies to give them a civilised burial, to get some closure on the past, to allow them to finally stop searching.

Then there are the nightmares for the parents who have a suspicion that their son has been involved in one of the country's high-profile cases. Some may make their peace with God as they get older and face their own mortality, but wouldn't it be a lot better to do it now, to lead Gardaí to the body at least?

Families of the missing do not have a problem with anonymous tip-offs through the Garda confidential line or through someone in a position of trust such as a priest or clergyman. And if someone were to tell it in confession there could be no comeback, not in this world anyway, whatever about the next. For the families of missing people, any kind of closure is welcome.

Missing Children

Most of the children who go missing in Ireland have in fact been snatched by a relative. In many cases, the child has been taken by an estranged parent, usually the father, and this has led to very difficult situations.

A lot of these incidents have occurred when a parent has reacted against a court order that has been made concerning the welfare of the child. The child is abducted and taken to another country where the laws may be very different from those in Ireland and, therefore, the Irish court order is very difficult to enforce.

In most missing children cases the child is returned unharmed after a short period of time. However, it has become a serious problem, so much so that there is now an organisation, founded by the Irish MEP Mary Banotti, to protect such children. It is called the Irish Centre for

Parentally Abducted Children (ICPAC) and is based in Dublin. The phone number is (01) 6620667.

A recent concern for parents has been the arrival of Internet chatrooms and the fact that it provides a very effective cover for paedophiles wanting to make contact with young people. There have been many cases of adults posing as young people on these sites and befriending children with the intent of eventually meeting them.

This year there have been some high-profile cases in both the UK and the US, where young girls have disappeared with older men who they met through a chatroom.

There are two high-profile cases of missing children in this country, those of Mary Boyle and Philip Cairns, neither of which has been solved despite the passage of years. A more recent disappearance was that of little Deirdre Crowley, who had been listed by her mother as missing for two years before being killed by her father. Sadly, there have been many other young children murdered over the years, but at least their families know what happened to them. The Boyle and Cairn families still have no answers.

Mary Boyle was almost seven years old when she disappeared at Cashelard, near Ballyshannon in Co. Donegal. Mary and her twin sister and older brother were born in England but, when the twins were two years old, their parents, Charlie and Ann, decided to return to Ireland as they thought it would be a better place to rear a family. On 18 March, 1977, Mary disappeared from a muddy boreen just yards from her grandparents' home.

There is a small memorial to the child near her home with a statue of a guardian angel and her photograph.

Philip Cairns was 13 years old in October 1986 when he vanished as he walked the short journey from his home back to school after lunch. His story is told in Chapter 27 of this book.

The Elderly

Elderly people disappear too. Many of them are suffering from some level of dementia and don't think that they are missing at all nor do they consider that they are doing anything outside their usual routine. Others are just forgetful and may go missing very close to home. These, of course, are the positive scenarios. Unfortunately, the elderly are also prey for fraudsters, robbers and attackers and that aspect always has to be investigated when the elderly go missing.

In the summer of 2003 there were two well-publicised searches for elderly people who went missing from home. In the first case, 91-year-old Joe Walsh disappeared in Lisronagh, near Clonmel, Co. Tipperary. He was found five days later in a cornfield, unharmed by his experience. Joe had been reported missing at lunchtime on Friday, 20 June, but the following Wednesday night he was found in a field less than a mile from his home by a sniffer dog. He was taken to St. Joseph's hospital for a check up and was treated for dehydration. He was in good shape but was slightly disoriented and had also suffered sunburn while out in the open. The fine weather and mild overnight temperatures helped to keep him alive.

The second case, involving an elderly woman, Nora Mary King, gave much cause for concern when her abandoned bicycle was found at the side of the road with no sign of her about. A few days later, she just knocked on the door of a neighbour's house, in good health and little the worse for wear. No one knows where she spent the previous few days or where she slept or if she ate. However, one theory is that she went to visit old friends in an area she remembered from long ago, but the houses in question are now derelict. You can read her story in Chapter 32.

Unfortunately some elderly people are not so lucky. Gardaí are still baffled by the disappearance of RTÉ's Alpho O'Reilly, who vanished somewhere between Dublin and Wexford in early January 1996. Alpho called to a garage in Ashford, Co. Wicklow at three o'clock in the morning and the kindly salesman realised he wasn't well and brought him in for a cup of tea. When he left, the salesman found he had left his credit cards behind and he ran after him. Alpho then asked which was the road to Dublin and was told to turn right. But instead he turned left, heading for Wexford. The salesman's father had died from Alzheimer's disease so he was very conscious of the dangers associated with an elderly man who seemed to be somewhat confused. He rang the Gardaí but they didn't respond swiftly enough to intercept Mr. O'Reilly.

The last reported sighting of him was in the village of Rathnew, when he knocked on a bed and breakfast establishment at four o'clock in the morning and asked if they had a bed for the night. Surprised by the lateness of the hour, the woman who opened the door was even more surprised when Alpho said he would like to see the room first. He inspected the room and told the woman he would let her know if he wanted it. He was never seen again.

The really strange thing is that his car, a very distinctive apple green Mitsubishi Colt, was never found either. His disappearance was featured on RTÉ's *Crimeline* on a number of occasions without any significant new information being uncovered. Of course, there is always the possibility that he left the country via Rosslare Harbour.

Suicides

Even the thought of suicide strikes fear in the hearts of family members. Some of those who are missing may have taken their own lives but their bodies have not been found. In other cases, bodies have been recovered. It must be remembered though that even if someone does leave a suicide note, it doesn't necessarily mean they are dead as they can change their mind at any time right up to the end.

Many of the young people who have been found dead left notes for parents and loved ones. The most tragic part of it is that, although a person may have felt that they couldn't go on any longer, the problem that sent them into this deep depression may not have lasted. It has to be accepted that suicide is not an easy option. The person who plans to take their own life is seriously ill, but the fact that it's not a physical ailment with blood and bandages makes it difficult to identify.

Some suicide victims take their lives quite openly; others hide away and that makes the discovery of their bodies so much more difficult. Witness the case of 27-year-old Derek Browne who left a suicide note when he went missing from Mullingar on 7 June, 2003. It was suspected that he had drowned in the canal but, almost three months later, he was found hanging from a tree close to the canal, but hidden behind a bush.

Along with the spate of suicides in Ireland, most of them young men, various counselling services have emerged. So, if you think someone you love is suffering in this way, you can get help for them. It may not chase their demons away immediately, but it will help them on the road to recovery. If you do notice a change in someone close to you, do not delay in looking for help for them.

The Wondering and the Waiting

One of the hardest things for the families of the disappeared is the knowledge that whenever a body is found, either exposed in bogland or woodland or washed up on a beach, there is the possibility that it is the remains of their loved ones.

Gardaí keep a record of any identifying marks, tattoos, scars or unusual features of all missing people and, through liaison with other police services, they try to match the body with a name. Dental records are often used as well although, since most records are only held for a certain length of time, they may not be available.

Obviously some bodies are harder to identify than others, particularly if they have been in water for some time. Even so, it is still surprising sometimes how long it can take before a friend or relative comes forward.

Forensic science has now made such strides that remains can nearly always be identified, although it can take some time. The family of Ellen Coss formally identified the remains of a woman washed up in the UK as their sister. They then waited a further six months for the results of DNA testing only to learn that the woman wasn't Ellen.

In May this year, a human foot was washed up on a beach in Dorset in England. Four months later, DNA testing proved it was that of a 14-year-old boy who had been missing from his home in Hampshire. The boy had disappeared after a fishing trip on New Year's Day 2002. The last sighting of him was on a pontoon over the River Hamble. When his fishing gear was found on the pontoon and he hadn't returned home, his parents raised the alarm. A search got underway but police believed that the boy had fallen into the river and been swept out to sea. The foot was found 40 miles away and, although it meant complete heartbreak for his family, it may yield some clue as to where the rest of his body is lying and experts are now studying the tides in the area. However, his family has stressed that the discovery tells them nothing about how their son disappeared.

It is important to understand that until a body is found, until tests can be carried out, families really don't know what happened or how a loved one died. This is one of the reasons that those who are guilty of abduction and murder don't want the body found. It would yield too much useful information, allowing forensic scientists to uncover quite a bit about those final hours and, most importantly, determine whether or not the body had met with a violent death. The discovery of a body can also yield invaluable material which can be matched with known suspects in the case.

Lost Contacts

There are missing people who don't suddenly disappear but who lose contact with their families over a period of time. Many of these are people who went abroad to work, didn't come home for holidays and started new lives and settled down elsewhere. There is nothing sinister in this, it's just something that happens often when elderly parents have died and the family home is sold. Coming home to a brother or sister isn't the same and doesn't carry the same urgency as a visit to a parent. When the family home is gone sometimes it's hard to keep the rest of the family in touch and the contacts melt away.

The Missing Persons websites have special sections for those who have lost contact with family or friends. Other useful sources are websites which reunite old school friends. Then there's the browsing option. One Dublin family recently made contact with a foster brother they hadn't seen for 40 years simply by putting his name and the details they had into the various search engines. One of the names matched a senior executive in a company in London and, more importantly, carried a photo as well. The family rang him the next day and made contact after so many years of not knowing where he was or what had become of him. They have picked up the threads of their lives and plan to stay in touch properly this time.

Birth Mothers

One of the most common type of searches in the world has to be those where people seek their birth mothers. They are not properly 'missing' but the children of these women often feel an acute loss. No matter how happy their lives have been and how successful their adoption, many people long to know their birth mothers, to know who their fathers were, why they were adopted and maybe to make contact with a wider extended family.

There are organisations that can help and some Missing Persons sites carry special sections for those who wish to contact their birth mothers and fathers.

Mike Greenwood was born in Galway in July 1951. He was baptised in the Parish of Rahoon, spent two years in a children's home and was then adopted by a family in the United States.

Mike's adoptive parents gave him a good home, but they died in 1982 when he was 31 years old. For more than 20 years now he has been trying to trace his family in Co. Galway. He has his birth certificate with his mother's name and other details, but hasn't been able to get over that final hurdle and actually make contact.

Mike has been going through local post offices trying to make contact with locals who might have the same surname as his birth mother. He has come close. Eighteen months ago, he almost succeeded in making contact with a man he thinks is his uncle, but this man died before the contact was made.

He told me: 'I think one day this will all work out. Even if she was found and did not want to see me, I can live with that. I have no "why" questions for her. I just want to let her know I'm doing fine and was well taken care of. I guess that's it.'

The Ones Who Come Back

People sometimes go missing for a few days and, despite their families often thinking the worst, they turn up again safely. This is especially traumatic in the case of teenagers. The fear of suicide is always there for the parents, as well as the awful feeling that there is something very wrong in the lives of their children. In the past several teenagers have disappeared but have come home again after a few weeks.

One mother told me how her 14-year-old son, Mark, went missing for one night and the sheer horror they went through imagining he had committed suicide. He returned home safely but twice went away again for a month at a time. There were no warnings, no messages left for anybody. His mother describes it as 'a living nightmare'. And yet the family are afraid to push the issue, to come down heavily on their son because they don't want to frighten him off completely or push him into doing something irrevocable.

His parents have nothing but praise for the Gardaí who helped to find him on all three occasions, but they say there should be more help out there for people like them, normal families who are going through crises with teenage children. They say that if there was more help available, a definite channel that parents knew about, then it might help teenagers in crisis and certainly might help to stem the number of suicides among young males.

'Our hearts go out to anyone who has a loved one missing and has never got them back; we can only imagine the horror of it. As a parent, it is a nightmare to lock your front door at night and not know where your son or daughter is.'

Visitors to Ireland

A number of those named among the disappeared were visitors to Ireland when they went missing. Some, like Bettina Poeschel from Germany, have been found murdered. Others, like Annie McCarrick and James Thompson, have just disappeared with no clues, no indication of where they are or what happened to them.

Another such mystery surrounds the disappearance of 59-year-old Gert Glader who went missing in Kildare on 16 May, 2002. The appeal for information on his disappearance was particularly urgent because he was in need of daily medication for a medical condition. It is believed that he could also have been using the name Mr B. Stahl. He holds an Austrian passport and had been staying in Kildare town although he had also lived in London. The day before he disappeared he made a cash withdrawal at an ATM machine.

The most recent search for a young overseas student who may be in Ireland is for Matt Mullaney from the United States. Matt is 21 and had been attending art school in Florence in Italy. But on 1 February he disappeared after leaving an Irish pub in Florence at 2.30 am. His parents say it is very much out of character for him to disappear like this. There was a sighting of him on a train from Dover to London on 5 April by a Dutch national. In conversation, Matt mentioned that he was going to spend some time in London before heading for Dublin where he was hoping to find work. Matt's parents have travelled from the US to Europe to search for him and they are typical of the many families asking the general public to keep an eye out for their son.

Missing Abroad

Several Irish people who have gone missing while overseas are still unaccounted for.

On 23 February, 2001, 36-year-old John Rowan from Monasterevin in Co. Kildare went missing from his home in Jacksonville, Florida in the United States. John was involved in the heavy equipment business and was also co-owner of Murphy's Pour House in St. Augustine. A month after he disappeared, police found his 1999 Ford Expedition in an office car park close to Orlando airport but it had been wiped clean of any forensic evidence.

Foul play is suspected but so far there is no evidence to suggest what might have happened to him. The Taoiseach, Bertie Ahern, helped to launch a poster campaign in the search for John while on a visit to the States. You can read more about the efforts of John's family to trace him in Chapter 8.

It is especially difficult for families when a loved one goes missing many miles from home in a totally different culture. This was what happened in the case of Dubliner Paul Roche, who disappeared in India in 1996. The 30-year-old was on the adventure of a lifetime, spending one and a half to two years trekking through the Himalayas on his own.

He was good at keeping in touch with his family and his girlfriend in Dublin, writing to them every three weeks or so until June 1996, when it all stopped. It is worth remembering too that this was seven years ago, before e-mail and Internet cafés had become a reality in even the busiest of cities. Today there are Internet cafés in the villages at many of the starting points where walkers, climbers and pilgrims enter the Himalayas, but it was a different scenario when Paul went missing.

Later, Paul's family found out that he still had US$800 in travellers cheques which were never cashed. At the time of his disappearance he was hiking through an area where a number of people have gone missing in recent years. There were suggestions at the time that Paul may have taken refuge in a mountain monastery but, despite extensive publicity and his inclusion on Missing Persons websites, there has been no news of him. His family are particularly anxious that other young Irish people travelling in the area be aware of Paul's disappearance and of what he looks like.

Brendan O'Riordan went missing in June 1995 when he was 25 years old. He comes from Templeogue in Dublin, but there is a possibility that he could be in either London or Sydney.

Brendan left to go to Australia on 27 June, 1995. Family and friends saw him off at Dublin airport for the first part of his journey, which would have taken him through London and then on to Sydney. He said that he would write when he arrived at his destination. He also told them that he had a job lined up in Sydney, which wouldn't have been difficult as Brendan is a qualified accountant and had already been to Sydney the previous December.

His family have not heard from him since the day he left Dublin airport. On 22 November of that year, 1995, Brendan's father died and his family are very concerned and desperately want him to get in touch.

It is not known whether he went on to Sydney or stayed in London and so the search concentrates on both Australia and England. Prior to leaving, Brendan closed all his bank accounts and credit card accounts. No one knows where he is but there was a suggestion that he could be in an area called Bowral, which is south west of Sydney between Goulburn and Sydney.

Then there is the case of Hugh Martin Nolan, a native of Blacklion in Cavan, who went missing from San Francisco in April 1994, just before his 22nd birthday. Hugh first went to the US in 1993, where he spent eight months living with his sister in New York. He then moved to San Francisco, where he lived in Judah and worked in the construction industry.

On the 20 April, 1994, he left his house and has not been seen since. He had just cashed a cheque in a downtown San Francisco bank for $500. His Irish passport has never been located (he would have needed this to cash the cheque and so it is assumed that he had it with him). Hugh's family, who live in Ireland, have been out to San Francisco a few times, but the distance makes it all the more difficult.

On 5 April, 2000, 48-year-old Dubliner Kieran Burke went missing in Yosemite Park in California. Kieran comes from Rathfarnham and was on a two-week holiday in San Francisco.

He travelled on to the Yosemite National Park where he had reserved accommodation from 4–5 April. He was last seen on 5 April in Yosemite Valley at Curry Village. He is described as 'adventurous' and would have had experience of hiking. There have been absolutely no clues as to his whereabouts or what happened to him. His rental car was left in a nearby parking lot.

The Park Rangers in Yosemite have been particularly active in searching for Kieran. Twenty-five employees and five dog teams were involved in the search and a helicopter was used to search steep cliffs around Nevada, Vernal and Yosemite Falls. It is thought that Kieran may have been planning a short one-day hike in the valley.

CCTV Cameras

The advent of closed-circuit television cameras on so many streets has assisted in identifying the movements of many missing people. They can be traced in shopping centres, along streets, at ATM machines or as they visit many business premises. But sometimes it ends in total frustration when somebody can be tracked for a while and then walks straight off camera. This was the case with Aengus Shanahan in Limerick city, who was picked up by cameras at a fast-food outlet and again leaving a night club, but then turned down a laneway and was never seen again.

It was also very frustrating in the case of 22-year-old Trevor Deely, who went missing in Dublin in December 2003. Trevor is from Naas in Co. Kildare, but he was living and working in Dublin at the time of his disappearance. He was last seen on Haddington Road and in the Leeson Street and Baggot Street areas early Friday morning, 8 December. It was a very windy wet night and it was in the middle of a taxi strike.

Trevor had been at a Christmas party earlier in the evening after which he returned to the bank where he worked in information technology. He was recorded on camera as he walked along with a blue golf umbrella. Video footage showed Trevor near Baggot Street Bridge at about 4.15 am and then, nothing.

Usually when someone disappears, business people are more than co-operative in making their CCTV footage available to Gardaí and the families of the missing people. However, it is important that this is requested immediately as film is often wiped and re-used. Despite the miles of footage being filmed at any one time, it is very frustrating when missing people's movements are not actually picked up anywhere.

Another photographic aid in trying to trace individuals comes from those using cameras and camcorders. Numerous appeals have been made in the cases of many different missing people. However, this needs to be done extremely quickly as well, as some of those filming may actually be visitors passing through.

What Do You Say To Them?

The families of the disappeared are in a sort of limbo, they are grieving the loss of their loved one while not knowing what exactly happened to them and still very definitely hoping they're going to be found safe and well.

So what do you say? What can you say? Sorrow seems premature and may even send out the message that you believe there is no hope of finding that person alive. Some families say people are afraid to talk to them, they don't know what to say. But one mother says she would like her friends and neighbours to behave normally, certainly to sympathise with her in the loss of her child, but also to dwell on anything positive they can think of, for example, any ongoing searches.

And don't stop trying to find the missing person. Offer to hand out fliers, to go round shops with a new handout, to e-mail friends overseas to make sure they pass the message on. But most of all, just be there.

The family of John Rowan, on their website dedicated to their search, express their gratitude 'for the compassion and love shown to us from family, friends and by many strangers. We are eternally grateful for your strength when we are weak, for your warmth when we are cold, for your laughter when we have none to share, for your stories of John that remind us that he is not forgotten. We thank God for you each and every day.'

I think that sums it up.

And Still It Goes On...

Almost every week someone 'new' goes on the Missing Persons website, although some of these entries are in the lost contacts category rather than that of people who have completely disappeared.

A recent arrival is a call for Maurice Gilmore to get in touch with his family. Maurice left his home in Belfast in 1982 and has not been seen or heard of since then. His brother, David, has appealed for help in contacting him as their 91-year-old mother is ill. Maurice is 53 years old and a qualified electrician. He was last seen in the Galway city area in 2001.

Another missing person listed is 25-year-old Stefan Punch, who has been missing from Cork city since 28 August, 2003. He was last seen at a friend's house in the city. His car was found the next day in Co. Clare. Since then, his mobile phone has been switched off and his friends and family have not had any word from him.

But, you know, there is good news too and some people are found safe and well. People sometimes sign the guest book on the Missing Persons website with their own good news and a message of hope.

A recent message came from Liam, who said he knows how the families of missing people feel. 'A while back my family couldn't trace a lost brother. Two weeks before our Mum died we managed to find him and get word to him. So all, please take note – don't give up hope. Pray, hope and don't worry.'

2

The Gardaí

Superintendent John Farrelly

The Gardaí place each missing person into one of three categories. 'A' is the most important. This describes an individual who is at immediate risk and would include the very young, those dependant on medicine, people for whom there is evidence to suggest that there could be a threat to their lives and those involved in known abductions. A new entry has crept into this category over the last couple of years, that of young illegal immigrants under 18 who have been put into care and then disappear. The bottom line is the immediate risk element, so alarm bells go off, a search gets underway and helicopters, dogs, sub aqua units, liaison with the media, house-to-house searches and even road blocks are part of the immediate operation.

It must be remembered that the vast majority of people do turn up eventually. In the year 2001, over 2,000 people went missing, the year before there were 1,800. This seems to be a huge number, but by the end of each year, most of them had turned up. Only about 20 people still hadn't been accounted for.

Then there are the 'B' and 'C' categories, which include people who have gone missing for a wide ranges of reasons, usually less abruptly; people who may have just decided to change their lifestyles. These are people who are over 18 years of age. Maybe they have lost their job, suffered a breakdown in a relationship or failed an exam. In some way there is a general sense of failure in what they are doing in a particular environment and they decide to change it, to make a difference, to start a new life.

Unfortunately, what actually happens is that they don't tell anybody and, in particular, they don't tell their nearest and dearest before they go. It is those people who are left behind that blame themselves and feel guilty. No matter how many times you tell them that there is no failure on their part, they still won't believe it until they get the news that their loved one has returned or that they are safe. Sometimes though they are not safe.

Superintendent John Farrelly joined An Garda Síochána 27 years ago. He is now the Garda Press and Public Relations Officer and spokesperson for the force and has had many experiences with missing persons cases. 'The family will have their own suspicions in relation to a loved one who may have changed their mood, their passions or the way they went about their daily lives. They may have had suicidal tendencies. Everybody thinks the worst in these cases and in a lot of them, the worst happens,' says John.

The race is to find these vulnerable people before anything happens to them 'and if you can get them on time perhaps you can save them and, on occasion, we have done. But the mind is a terrible thing with people and unfortunately, even in the recent past, we have had to pull missing people out of water or in various different circumstances.' When a missing person does commit suicide, 'it is a hugely sad time for the family and there is always the guilt associated with it, the wondering if they could have somehow prevented it'.

John says the first thing to do when you suspect a person is missing is to make contact with the Gardaí and give them as much information as possible. And how long should you wait? Each case is different. He says that some families know there is a problem within minutes of a loved one going out. John recalls being contacted by a family who were alarmed when their father went for a walk without the dog. In that case, the worst did happen, but the family knew immediately something was wrong when he uncharacteristically went out alone without the family pet.

The Gardaí will take a report seriously, he stresses, so just rely on your own knowledge of the situation, of the person concerned and of their behaviour. If there is anything unusual happening and somebody cannot be found, raise the alarm.

The best way to get in touch with the Gardaí is through the local station or, if not open 24 hours, the nearest round-the-clock Garda station.

And John warns that 'the Gardaí will question you to annoyance, they will ask personal questions and the whole idea is to be as truthful as possible. Don't put the Gardaí on the wrong trail by trying to cover up something or by thinking you have to give the missing person a wonderful character reference. The more we know of the person, the better chance we have of finding them.'

The Garda press office regularly issues appeals for missing people. Many of them are only missing for a few hours or overnight. There have been recent high-profile cases of young people disappearing of their own accord. In those circumstances the Gardaí work to get them home safely, generally watching airports and seaports and train stations.

There have also been a number of cases of elderly persons disappearing from home. Some of these people are suffering from senility and are very vulnerable away from home. In all of these cases, it is essential that the alarm is raised as soon as possible, so that the search can begin.

3

The Missing Persons Website

Fr Aquinas Duffy

On 11 February, 2000, Aengus Shanahan from Limerick city went missing. (You can read his story in Chapter 11 of this book.) Fr Aquinas Duffy, Aengus' cousin, came up with the idea of setting up a website to help find Aengus and also to assist the families of other missing persons. The website, www.missing.ws, has now grown and carries details of dozens of missing people as well as lost contact listings, people trying to trace their birth mothers and photos of the disappeared.

Over the years, a number people have been found; some were deceased and some alive. Let me quote from the website: 'For those who were deceased, we pray that they rest in peace. For those alive, we pray that they live their lives to the full. For all their families, whether their loved ones were found alive or dead, their nightmare has ended and they have at least the comfort that their loved ones are no longer "missing".'

To date in the missing persons section of this website, 40 people have been found, 18 of them alive and 22 deceased.

In the lost contact section, 73 families have been reunited or found information, some after searching for over 50 years.

Fr Aquinas explained that he got involved after Aengus went missing: 'I wanted to do something to try to find him. I wanted to try and get him posted on an Internet website, but I discovered that there weren't any websites for Ireland. So I started one, for Aengus initially, and then I opened it up to everybody else and that's how the Irish Missing Persons website was born.'

But what constitutes a missing person? 'I suppose it's anybody who just doesn't come home, particularly under suspicious circumstances when they hadn't made any obvious plans to go away. Effectively they've just vanished and usually it is totally out of character for that person not to return home. That is a missing person.'

Fr Aquinas is acutely aware of the trauma suffered by the families of the disappeared. 'Prior to Aengus going missing I certainly didn't understand what it meant to have a family member disappear, it's actually a term which really doesn't adequately describe the kind of grief and trauma and utter devastation that a whole family go through. There's guilt and the frustration, even not knowing where to start. Initially you might go around ringing friends to try and find out where the person is, to see if anybody has any information. Then you're into posters, then you're into press appeals, and as time goes on it becomes more and more difficult as you grow more and more anxious for the safety of the person.'

But Fr Aquinas is positive on the eventual outcome for most families. He says the vast majority do turn up safe and sound. 'They don't necessarily return home, which I think is important to state, but most of them do make contact with somebody who can identify them. They tell them "I'm okay but I'm not coming home". Then, at least, the family knows they're safe and the searching can end.'

Quite a few missing people do return home, but there is a small percentage who remain untraced at the end of a year, 'what happens to them we don't know until they're found either dead or alive'.

And Fr Aquinas agrees with the families and all those who have searched for the missing in saying that there are people out there who know something about their loved one's disappearance or indeed who may have participated in that disappearance.

'Certainly in a number of cases I am convinced there are people, maybe even people who are reading this, who have the missing pieces of information. They could bring an end to the suffering of a family by coming forward and saying yes, they do know and I always would appeal to them to come forward because if they knew for even one second the pain and trauma that they are actually putting a family through over months and years, I believe they would reveal what they know. If they could even get a taste of what a family is actually suffering as a result of the disappearance, they would come forward.'

But even if the news is bad, even if the loved one has died in the meantime, it is important that the family knows what has happened to them.

'I think at the end of the day people want to know what happened, they want the answer to that question and until a person is found either dead or alive that search will continue. Of course you always live in hope because you can't take hope from people, so until a person is found people will tend to think positively. They hope that maybe somebody will come forward and say yes, the person is here or, indeed, as has happened in some cases, the missing person has literally walked in the front door after being away for a few months much to the shock and surprise and joy, but also the anger, of their family.'

However, until the missing person is found, one way or another the search goes on. 'This is the problem; you get some families who are left for years and years in this limbo.'

Even though it might be suspected that someone has been abducted or murdered, an actual murder investigation cannot even begin until a body is found. Fr Aquinas says that it is important that the law is changed in Ireland in this respect, particularly where there are suspicious circumstances surrounding a person's disappearance. 'I know that in some cases in America where there are suspicious circumstances, from day one they are gathering forensic evidence, be it hair samples from their home or the last known place where the person disappeared. Something like this can be very important and useful later on, but in Ireland, unfortunately, you can't have a murder investigation until you have a body, so even years and years later if a body is found, only then will a murder investigation start and of course it's often too late in many respects at that stage.'

So how do you get a missing person on the website?

Just make contact with the website and Fr Aquinas will do the rest. And don't forget the Garda website as well. The Gardaí have a special leaflet which carries the names and addresses of the relevant organisations which will be useful.

Fr Aquinas cautions, however, that things are sometimes not quite what they seem when it comes to the disappeared. 'For instance, you might have a case when somebody's gone missing and subsequently their car is found parked near a beach or near a cliff and everybody automatically presumes that it has to be a suicide. But it's not always so. There have been cases where such a person has subsequently made contact, not with their family, but with somebody else. In some cases it would appear that parking the car on the cliff or leaving a neat pile of clothes on a beach was just a very elaborate plan to make people think they were dead. Sometimes they have gone to start a new life somewhere else.'

And missing people sometimes access the website themselves. Fr Aquinas has had one or two who made contact with him after seeing themselves posted as missing. 'It doesn't happen that often', he says, 'but one or two have contacted me directly and asked me to pass on a message to their family. There was one case when a person from Ireland who was missing abroad actually saw one of his own posters on a pole which had been printed off from my website and he contacted home then.'

Fr Aquinas stresses the importance of speed when you suspect someone has disappeared. 'Where you are concerned for the safety of the person, particularly when the disappearance is totally out of character, it is very important to have a public appeal from day one. I always think that the first 24 hours are important because we desperately need the help of the public to be the eyes and ears out there in as many places as possible.'

And yes, some families do have personal issues that they might not want to see aired publicly. There may have been a row or a marriage breakdown, but they can still publicise the disappearance without disclosing personal information.

'The main thing is to get a public appeal underway so the details you are publicising include the person's photograph, height, the colour of their hair etc. There is certainly no question of the personal details of a family being revealed. That's personal and the family have a right to their privacy.'

Fr Aquinas also advises families to work closely with the Gardaí and the media in making public appeals 'and to remain hopeful. Often people at the very start think the worst, but I think it is important to remember that out of over 2000 that go missing every year, 98 per cent of them are found. Families must remember that.'

Every day he prays for Ireland's missing people and, although there isn't a specific patron saint for them, Fr Aquinas says 'I have kind of chosen St Joseph because when he was 12 years old, Jesus went missing for three days and his parents had the experience of missing their child. They were frantic but they also had the joy of finding him as well, so I often think that Joseph and Mary are the patrons of missing people and their families.'

Fr Aquinas Duffy

4

Helpful Organisations

The National Missing Persons Helpline

The National Missing Persons Helpline has been running since October 2002. It is funded by the Department of Justice, Equality and Law Reform and provides a counselling and advice service for the families and friends of missing people.

Tony O'Connell runs the service. First there's the Helpline, which operates Monday to Friday from 9.30 am to 5.00 pm. Outside these hours and at weekends you can leave a message which will be accessed during office hours.

Tony explains that the service does not actually go about finding people. 'We don't trace missing people, our first aim is to provide information to family and friends on organisations that can help them. We can put them in touch with people who can help with the practicalities and we can listen.'

Tony says a lot of people feel they have no one to talk to after a loved one goes missing, 'especially when time passes and the missing person may not be the general topic of conversation anymore, but they need to talk and we're here to listen.'

The Helpline can also act as the co-ordinator between the family and the Gardaí. Tony stresses that anyone is welcome to get in touch with them whether the loved one has been missing for a few hours or even for many years. 'There is still trauma and upset to be dealt with', he says. One of the families the Helpline worked with was trying to cope 60 years after someone went missing.

The Helpline is situated in the Offices of Victim Support at 32 Arran Quay, Dublin 7. The phone number is 1850 442 552 and the e-mail is missingpersons@victimsupport.ie. Tony advises that the phone option is the best way of making contact.

The London Irish Centre

For the past 17 years the London Irish Centre has been providing a most efficient service in searching for missing Irish people in the UK. It is the only Irish organisation in Britain that operates such a service. Over the last 10 years, 625 people have been located and reunited with their families. The success rate is around 42 per cent.

The centre acknowledges that families lose touch for a number of reasons. In the past, emigration was a huge contributing factor. Family disputes and disagreements also contributed to this sad outcome and still do. A generation passes and the break can seem irretrievable. However, a change of spirit, new life experiences, a chance encounter with the past or a bereavement may act as a catalyst in the quest to find a lost relative.

Their website www.irishcentre.org is well laid out and has an online application form for those seeking their assistance. The centre says that it is vital that as much information as possible be included on this form 'because a search can only be as good as the information provided'. They warn, however, that 'without a date of birth, any search is impossible'. The initial search takes about two months, then, depending on how that goes, a further search is instigated.

The results vary from failure to make contact, to the missing person refusing to acknowledge the enquiry or acknowledging the enquiry but refusing to allow a re-connection of the lost link. The missing person can be hesitant about re-establishing the link with their past and a process of liaison through an intermediary can take place over a period of time.

The service is completely confidential and should a person be found, the choice is theirs as to whether to re-establish contact or not. The service warns that 'the person searching has to accept the outcome'. However, before you fill in the form you should be aware that there are a number of limitations. Some of the enquiries they don't handle are those involving debt collection, natural parents seeking their adopted children or vice versa or those trying to trace missing people for social rather than welfare reasons.

5

John McGuinness TD

'The families were living in limbo.'

John McGuinness, TD for Carlow and Kilkenny, is deeply committed to the campaign to secure better training and resources for the police and those working to find missing people in Ireland. Based on fact-finding trips he has made to the US, he is urging professionals there to make a case study of a missing Irish person, believing the findings would introduce new ideas and experience to the search for missing people in Ireland. On a trip to the States with Mary and Martin Phelan, Jo Jo Dullard's sister and her husband, in March 2003, John received Hillary Clinton's political support for their fact-finding mission. Hillary was particularly interested given that New York citizen, Annie McCarrick, went missing in Ireland.

The trauma and unending sadness which plagues the families of missing people affected Deputy John McGuinness back in 1996 when he was Lord Mayor of Kilkenny. 'Jo Jo Dullard went missing in 1995. Her family are from Kilkenny and her sister came to me at the time. The extent of the families' suffering was something I wasn't aware of but their lobbying drew my attention – how they could be so driven? I began to see how lives were affected by someone who had gone missing. The families were living in limbo, not even having a body. The trauma and unending sadness encouraged me into it.'

John used his position as a TD to further the cause of missing people when he was elected to the Dáil in 1997. He arranged a meeting with the Taoiseach, Bertie Ahern, whom he says was quite taken by the experience. 'He began to query things for me and to assist Mary Phelan. Mary and Bertie have become quite good friends now, during the election campaign in Kilkenny he took time out to meet with the Phelans.'

John says he has succeeded in convincing the Taoiseach to set time aside in his busy schedule to work on the campaign for missing people. 'Bertie has asked me to meet with the missing people lobby and to do a progress report.'

John says there now exists a 'loose coalition' between himself, Mary Phelan and others involved in the goal to establish cohesive institutions and introduce measures to assist in finding people who go missing in Ireland.

The trip to America was an eye-opener for Deputy McGuinness; the professional, highly-organised approach in the States highlighting the shortcomings of services in Ireland. The group visited the Centre for Missing and Exploited Children in Washington, where they were given insight into how 70,000 missing cases were solved through the work of the organisation. The new techniques and the use of information technology in locating missing persons impressed them. 'They explained how they have employed 17,000 professionals and trained them in these techniques. The FBI is involved as well.'

The Centre in Washington trains people and organisations that play a role in searching for missing people. They train volunteers along with members of the police force, so they know how to approach the situation when someone is reported missing.

On the trip to the States, John discovered that the service offers a free training service to the Irish police. 'They have set up a Gerry

McCabe fellowship in honour of murdered Detective Garda Gerry McCabe. The fellowship furnishes an exchange service between Ireland and the USA to skill members up in police techniques.' John McGuinness has now received written confirmation that in spring 2004, two members of An Garda Síochána will participate in training at the Centre for Missing and Exploited Children and Adults in Washington.

The Garda Commissioner has also approved Ireland's participation in a 13-country website for missing people, which is also driven by the Centre for Missing and Exploited Children and Adults. A further successful outcome of the trip to the US is that the Gardaí will now remain in contact with the centre in Washington, in order to keep up to date with the training courses available with a view to participation.

In America, Hillary Clinton has put protocols and initiatives through the senate on what should be done when someone goes missing. Included among these protocols is 'Amber Alert'. This flashes lights across the highway screens, with messages alerting all drivers when somebody goes missing. While the Irish group was in the US in March, President Bush also enacted 'Code Adam', another of Hillary Clinton's protocols. 'Code Adam' covers instructions on how action should be taken in various places such as large department stores or supermarkets when somebody goes missing.

These protocols are devised by people in Hillary Clinton's office, people who are specifically involved with what is required in the area of missing persons. These officials told John they would be happy to come to Ireland and talk to the police force here and explain what should be done. Since President Bush signed Code Adam into legislation, department stores are legally obliged to inform staff of the methodology of dealing with this type of situation if it arises. 'They are much more organised in the States. They are very person-specific. Designated people know that they each have an individual task, for example, one step they must follow is to advise the police in the area.

The police in turn trigger action. This could even be Amber Alert if the person has left the department store.'

The Irish group were witness to a person being found after 14 years while they were over there. John McGuinness, along with Mary and Martin Phelan, could see how well-organised the searches for missing people were in America and returned to Ireland determined to take some of their techniques on board.

They met with the Taoiseach and the Minister for Justice and presented their findings to them. They particularly emphasised the facility already in place, under which the Irish Police Force could gain from the American experience by undergoing training. Deputy McGuinness regarded it as annoying and frustrating that private citizens were the ones who had to do the work when police forces have the resources to share information and procedures as a matter of course. He feels that following the meeting they were left with the understanding that the Department of Justice would pursue the matter 'with a positive and pro-active approach'. 'They are going to consider the offers of training available to them.'

Deputy McGuinness wants to see the government and the police take a more pro-active approach in Ireland. He finds it disappointing that all the work Mary Phelan does has to be helped along by sponsorship. It was an American airline that sponsored her trip to the US in March, while John McGuinness paid for his trip himself. It was a very worthwhile experience nonetheless. He sees Mary Phelan's role as invaluable, given that she understands the plight facing the families of missing people. 'She connects with other families and understands what it is like for them and is therefore in a position to highlight the situation facing them.'

The trip to the States has presented plenty of new ideas that could be implemented in Ireland. 'We will continue to press the case further. I try to make it clear in every interview that we are never giving up. I want to see tangible developments.'

After almost seven years of being involved with the campaign, John McGuinness's trip to the US has led to his suggestion of the 'Irish case-study' idea. 'I suggested the professionals in the states take a case similar to that of Jo Jo Dullard and arrive at an Irish prototype, so we'll gain from their experience and know what to do in an Irish scene. We can't have all the structures that they have in the US, but this could make a huge difference.'

John McGuinness, TD

Mary and Martin Phelan

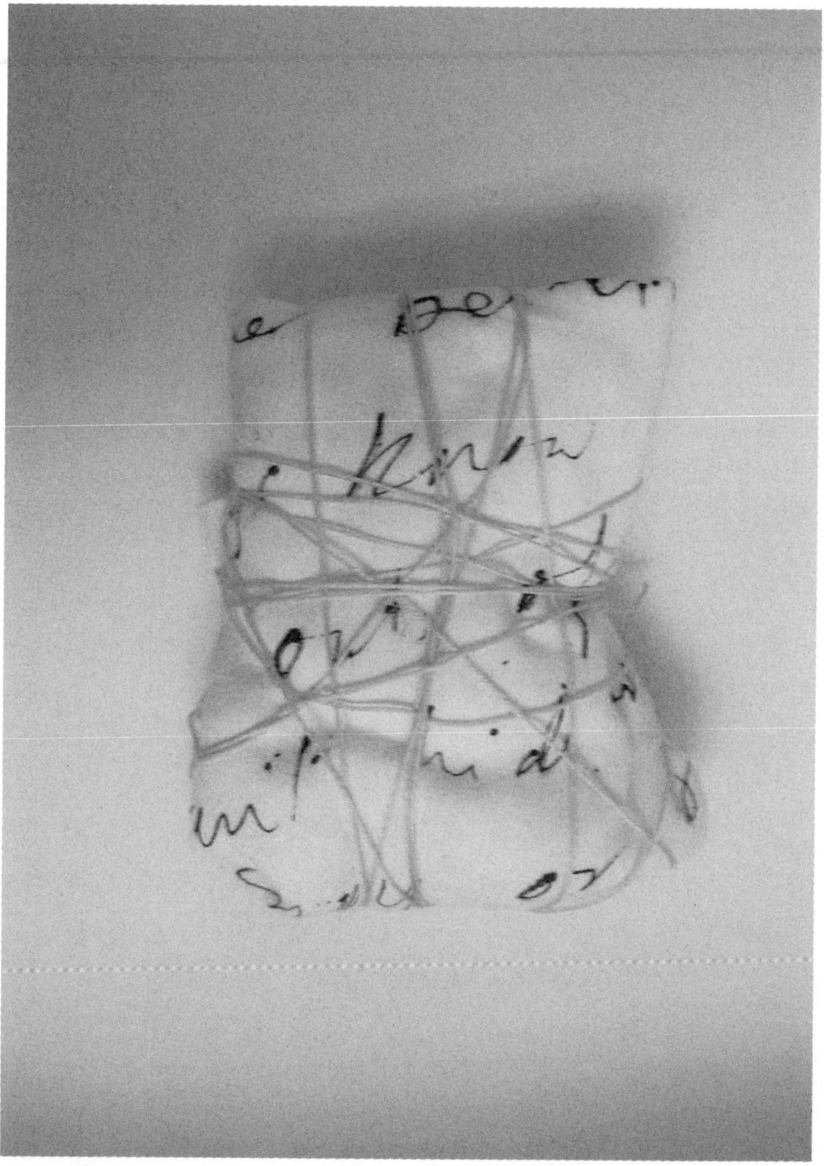

6

Wills O'Brien

'I want my daddy to come home.'

Born January 1960.
Missing from Buttevant, Co. Cork since 23 April, 2002.

While most seven-year-old girls are thinking about Barbie dolls and endless other toys when discussing their lists for Santa Claus, the 2002 Christmas wish of Natalie O'Brien in Charleville, Co. Cork was for just one thing: 'I want my Daddy to come home.'

Natalie's father, Wills O'Brien, has been missing from Buttevant, Co. Cork since April 2002. His wife, Patricia, and little Natalie, are distraught and out of their minds with worry, not knowing what has happened to him.

Wills O'Brien disappeared very suddenly. The circumstances surrounding his disappearance are unusual and difficult to comprehend. He was last seen in the early hours of the 23 April, 2002, when a friend dropped him off after an evening out.

Wills had been staying on his parents' farm in Buttevant for a few weeks prior to his disappearance and had been working the day he went missing. He was in the marquee hire business and travelled around the countryside to meet clients. The evening of his disappearance, Wills finished up work at 5 pm and parked his car in the town. He then dropped in on a publican friend of his who was working at the time. The publican noted that Wills was troubled that evening. In the course of their conversation Wills told him he felt that he was being followed and was clearly agitated. The publican was giving Wills a lift home shortly after 2 am when Wills asked him to stop, saying that he needed to go to the toilet. He asked his friend to let him off beside a field on the way. Wills then got out of the car and told his friend to go on, that he would make his own way home through the fields. That was the last time Wills was ever seen.

Two days later, Wills' wife, Patricia O'Brien, received a phone call. It was a friend of Wills' in Buttevant, who was ringing to say that Wills was officially missing and the police had been notified. There has been neither sight nor sound of Wills since. Patricia received a nasty shock on hearing the news. As she heard the details surrounding Wills' disappearance, she was more and more bewildered. There was no history of Wills feeling persecuted, and Patricia was very disturbed when she heard about his agitated mood that night. She couldn't understand why he hadn't made it home after being dropped off and was highly concerned for her husband's safety.

It certainly didn't look like Wills had planned to take off. He hadn't taken a change of clothes with him or packed any belongings, when last seen he was wearing a navy fleece jumper, black trousers and brown boots. He didn't have a passport, so if he did travel, it is unlikely that he went any further than the UK. His car was found parked in the Main Street of the town where he had left it.

Patricia doesn't believe Wills would have gone off of his own accord: 'It just wasn't in his nature. He had never done anything like it before.' What utterly convinces her that Wills' disappearance could not have been in any way planned is the fact that he was crazy about his daughter, Natalie, and he wouldn't leave her without saying anything. She knows there is no way he would leave his beloved six-year-old daughter without any explanation. Natalie's seventh birthday was just over a week after Wills went missing and Patricia had hoped that he would show up on the day. 'He was crazy about Natalie. She was a real Daddy's girl.'

The Gardaí launched a search in Buttevant. Wills had lots of friends, both in Buttevant and Charleville, and they all took part in the search. Posters were put up and the search team went through the streets and fields looking for any sign of Wills. The story also appeared on RTÉ's *Crimeline.* Following the airing of Wills' story there was a huge number of phone calls. There were many reported sightings and there was even one man who was convinced he had taken a lift in a car driven by someone matching Wills' description. All leads were thoroughly investigated but turned up nothing; his disappearance remains a total mystery.

The traumatic experience of not knowing where Wills is has put Patricia under huge strain and she doesn't know what to think. While her gut feeling is that he is out there somewhere, the fact that he is not making any effort to make contact his family, especially his young daughter, does not make any sense.

'I think he's still alive but then at times I can't help but wonder if he is dead.' She bursts into tears: 'If he's alive, how could he do this, how could he do this to Natalie?' Patricia's head is completely confused with different theories of what could have happened. 'The problem is that none of them add up. I know Wills! We were married for seven years. I know he would not commit suicide and anyway, if he did commit suicide, surely they would have found a body at this stage... But then, if he's not dead, where is he?' The situation is distressing.

David Linehan, one of the founders of the Missing Persons Association in Ireland, also brought a search team in. David had a lot of experience looking for people who went missing in similar situations to Wills, ever since he got involved in the movement following the disappearance of his own father. Their team also met with blanks.

Wills' disappearance is extremely confusing as it makes no sense whatsoever. At the time of his disappearance, Patricia had been married to Wills for seven years and prior to that had been going out with him for four, having met him in a disco. One of his strong character traits was his extremely relaxed attitude to life. He wasn't inclined to get worked up about little things and people were drawn to him by his easy-going personality. She says he was a very jolly type, extremely laid back with a 'devil-may-care' attitude, and everybody loved him. 'He wouldn't get into a panic about anything', she recalls. Wills had loads of friends throughout the country, a lot of whom he met through work. Patricia contacted all of these people in the hope that they may have seen or heard from Wills but, like everyone else, they had nothing to report and were taken aback at the news that he was gone. 'They were shocked.'

The guards told Patricia that they believe he has gone away somewhere, but they do not know where. They did point out that 'people have the right to go missing'. Patricia understands this, but the question she keeps asking herself is 'where could he have gone with no passport?' She can't fathom how he could have vanished so totally. There was nowhere she could imagine he could have gone as 'he had never been out of the country'.

The families of missing people will explore every avenue if they believe there is even a slight chance of finding their loved ones. After the Garda search, the poster campaign and the coverage on *Crimeline* brought them no closer to finding Wills – Patricia decided to call in an Irish psychic. She was careful in her choice and went on friends' recommendations. She e-mailed a couple of psychics and one of them got back to her. It took the psychic a month before she came back with her feelings as to where Wills could be. Over the month, Patricia also forwarded details of the case to a psychic over in England to see if there was any sign over there. The Irish psychic eventually came back to Patricia. She said Wills was alive and he was around boats. She also said that he would not be back for a long time. The psychic did not ask for any money for her help, and Patricia trusts that she is genuine. However, she knows you can never be sure, psychics can often be wrong and it would be a mistake to completely rely on the information and take it for fact.

It is very important to have the support of family and friends when going through the nightmare of a loved one disappearing. Patricia has found huge support in her own family since Wills' disappearance. The subject comes up every day, with someone always wondering afresh where he could have got to. Patricia and Natalie moved into Patricia's parents' home once they heard the shocking news that Wills was missing. They have stayed there ever since. 'My family are brilliant. They have been extremely supportive', she says.

The most difficult moments for Patricia arise when Natalie starts asking questions. She cried herself to sleep for nights on end, sobbing 'I want my Daddy'. Patricia did not know how to explain to the six-year-old that her father was missing, but then Natalie came home from school one day with the news. Her classmates had told her that her father was a missing person, after hearing adult conversation about it. Natalie was very distressed and imagined all kinds of horrible things had happened to him. 'She's a child, she thought her father had got lost and couldn't find his way home from the fields.' But Natalie brings the subject of her father's disappearance up less and less as time goes on. 'But she still talks about him to friends, saying "my Daddy does this and that". She misses him a lot as they used to spend lots of time together. Wills brought his daughter everywhere with him. He would bring her to his family's farm and to see horses. Wills would do anything for Natalie. He was crazy about her.'

Patricia is convinced there is someone out there who knows what happened to her husband and pleads with anyone with any information to come forward. It is impossible that nobody knows anything. As time goes on, part of her feels she is never going to find out what happened to him, leaving her in a limbo that makes living an ordinary life very hard. She is determined to try and get on with life, however, for her own sake and for Natalie's. It is very difficult though, as she wakes up every day with the lingering question: 'Where is he?' Patricia would love to have answers, to know what happened, to have closure. In the meantime, she does her best to cope: 'I take each day as it comes. I hope he's alright. I always hope I'll hear something, just to know that he's okay.'

Though she can't imagine that he is hiding away of his own accord, she accepts it could be a possibility, despite how out of character it would be for a man she knew so well. 'If he is out there, I'll never forgive him though. I'll never forgive him for putting me through this, for putting Natalie through this. It's not fair when there's a child involved.' Wills has missed 18 months of Natalie's life. As each day passes and Natalie gets older, he is not part of her growing up, and the longer this goes on, the more it seems like it will go on forever. Patricia does not know whether her little girl will see her father before she becomes an adult, or whether she will ever get to have a conversation with him as an adult. The worst fear imaginable is that Natalie will never again see the man who helped bring her into this world, the man she loved so much, the daddy who took her everywhere.

Natalie will be making her first Holy Communion next year. Neither she nor Patricia know whether the event will be witnessed by her proud father.

7

Michael Anthony Lynch

'The heating was on, the bedside lamps were lighting.'

Born 1 August, 1947.
Missing from Clones, Co. Monaghan since 6 January, 2002.

'I do love you and I do love the children but I'll never be back.'

That was the last chilling phone call from Tony Lynch to his wife, Angela, shortly after midnight on 5 January, 2002. Two days later he disappeared.

It hadn't been much of a Christmas for the family, 'lonesome' was how Angela described it. They had been having problems and Tony had left his home in Newtownbutler in November 'to sort himself out'. He went to live in a flat over the border in Clones, Co. Monaghan, which was his address until he went missing. His family says Tony had his problems, he was a binge drinker and suffered from depression.

Tony would now be 56 years old. Angela, his wife, is 18 years his junior.

Despite his problems, Tony continued to go to work. He worked with heavy machinery and was close friends with his employer. He had a reputation as a hard worker. That year, he worked right up to Christmas. And, although he sent Angela the money for Christmas, he decided not to return home.

After Christmas, Tony was seen in a local pub. People who knew him said he was clean shaven and well dressed and only had two drinks.

Later, Tony's brother called to his flat in Clones but couldn't get an answer. Fearing he had fallen or was ill, he got into the flat, but there was no sign of Tony and there was no indication that he had planned to go away. Nothing was missing. The heating was on, the bedside lamps were lighting and his mobile phone was charging. Even his razor was left behind. 'To me it looked like he had gone out for a few drinks and never intended to stay away'. Angela says, 'it didn't look like a place where somebody was planning to leave'.

The alarm was raised and a search began. Tony had taken his car, a white Mitsubishi Galant, and for a time the search concentrated on finding the car. A search of the local lakes got underway from the air but neither Tony nor the car were ever found.

The next problem Angela faced was what to tell her children. They knew their dad had gone away for a bit but they were expecting him back and how do children understand the concept of somebody disappearing? When Tony went missing the three boys were aged 18, 14 and 12 and his daughter, the little girl described by her mum as 'the little lassie, Daddy's girl', was 10.

And while the search goes on, Angela has found it hard to cope with the fact that the fuss has died down. 'For the first couple of weeks after Tony disappeared, the house was full', she says, 'but now there's nobody there. You can't believe it when this comes to your own door, the unpleasantness of it.'

And where is Tony? Angela doesn't know what to think. 'Lots of days I get up and I think he's dead and that makes it easier; then I wake up the next day and I think he is alive out there somewhere.'

Part of her wants to believe that Tony is still alive and well and that he could still be part of the children's lives.

She has consistently appealed: 'If anybody knows where Tony is, for the sake of the four wee ones, they just need to know. Otherwise, we can't move on, I can't tell the children their daddy is dead or he's not coming back when I don't know what happened. You can't mourn, part of you has to keep alive for the kids. We talk about him often.'

Despite all the trauma and the fact that he had left the family home at the time of his disappearance, Angela insists her husband is 'a good person. He never did anyone any harm. He is quiet, shy at times. I've no doubt he loved me and loved them.'

8

John Rowan

'They have a picture of their daddy under their pillows.'

Born 25 August, 1966.
Missing from Jacksonville, Florida since 23 February, 2001.

On 23 February, 2001, 36-year-old John Rowan from Monasterevin in Co. Kildare went missing from his home in Jacksonville, Florida in the United States. John was involved in the heavy equipment business and was also co-owner of Murphy's Pour House in St. Augustine.

A month after he disappeared, police found his 1999 Ford Expedition in an office car park close to Orlando airport, but it had been wiped clean of any forensic evidence. Foul play is suspected but so far there is no evidence to suggest what might have happened to him. The Taoiseach, Bertie Ahern, helped to launch a poster campaign in the search for John while on a visit to the US.

John's family have set up a very comprehensive website which includes updates on the case as well as a photo gallery, but John's disappearance is complicated. A handwriting expert hired by police believes that his signature was forged on a form that transferred his $3 million in life insurance benefits from his family to his business partners. Ten months before his disappearance, the beneficiaries of the policy were changed from his family to his partners in his land development company.

However, the policy is just one aspect of a case that has baffled investigators and Rowan's family since the day he went missing. John is a family man but he has missed both his children's birthdays and his eight-year-old daughter Alycia's first Holy Communion. He is described on his website as a 'doting father and husband who would call home numerous times a day'.

John's wife, Caroline, says she is clinging to the hope that he is alive somewhere, maybe suffering from amnesia. 'I have to, in my heart, believe that he is still alive', she says, 'I need him to come home soon.' But others, including the police, fear the worst. This is bolstered by the length of time John has been missing and how out of character it is for him not to call his family and business associates. His bank accounts and mobile phone haven't been touched since he disappeared at about 5 am, the usual time he left for work, yet there is no physical evidence that he is injured or dead.

Detectives have spent most of their time digging through bank and phone records. Sergeant Scott McLeod of the Jacksonville Sheriff's Office Missing Persons Unit describes it as 'tedious, frustrating work'.

Since John's disappearance, his family has blanketed the city with hundreds of thousands of fliers, hired a private investigator and offered a reward, and their Internet site has received hundreds upon hundreds of messages of support from around the world. Family and friends have flown out from Ireland to join parishioners, neighbours and friends in the search. Their neighbourhood is dotted with green and yellow ribbons as a gesture of support.

John's parents, Margaret and John Senior, met with Taoiseach Bertie Ahern to ask for his help, as there have been no leads. 'We don't think the detectives have gotten a dozen calls', Caroline says.

John Rowan Jnr went to the United States from Monasterevin in Co. Kildare 15 years ago during the recession in Ireland. He helped build several construction businesses and was a partner in a pub in St. Augustine. His parents went to live there too and settled just around the corner in Chasewood.

The night before he disappeared, John hosted a barbeque for family and friends at his home. His wife last saw him when she woke up briefly at 3 am.

The next possible sighting was when two neighbourhood girls told police they saw his truck leaving the neighbourhood about the time John usually left for work, but, because of the tinted windows, they couldn't say who was inside. He was supposed to call his sister to wake her up for school because his parents were on a cruise, but he never made that call. He also failed to show up at the airport that night to collect his parents. 'We always knew where he was', says his mother, 'now it seems no one does.'

But his family clings to hope. Every night, before bed, John's son Robert mouths a six-year-old's prayer: 'Please Daddy, hurry, hurry, hurry, hurry, hurry home to us.'

'He keeps saying as many hurries as he can', says his mum, Caroline, 'The children have a picture of their daddy under their pillows and I make sure they talk to him every night'.

The search for John and their faith in his eventual return keeps the family going. 'The time spent without John has been difficult and soul wrenching. Our son, brother, husband and father is missing; a remarkable individual who touched many people and warmed many hearts.' They say they have been blessed by many shoulders to cry on and support them.

9

Sandra Collins

'She went down town for a message and never came back.'

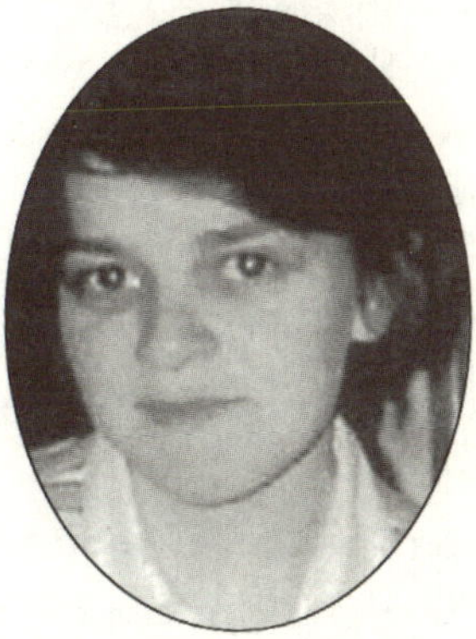

Born 1971.
Missing from Killala, Co. Mayo since 4 December, 2000.

Killala in Co, Mayo is a small town. Sandra Collins once told her sister, Bridie Conway, that to be really accepted there, you had to be born and bred there or have your roots in the locality for a least a century. When Sandra left school, she went to live with her aunt Ann in Ballina and had a part-time job in the area. Ann suffered from very severe arthritis from the age of 22 and, as it became progressively worse, the young Sandra gave up her part-time job and became her aunt's carer. The two got on very well together and, in 1990, aunt Ann moved to live in Killala and Sandra went with her.

On 4 December, 2000, around 7.30 pm, Sandra went down the town for a message. She went to the shop and bought sausages, but didn't return home. The last sighting of her was around 11 pm that evening in the local chip shop. She was only a couple of minutes walk away from home.

According to her sister Bridie, Sandra is a quiet person. Her hobbies are reading and walking and she was good at keeping in touch with Bridie and with her mother who lived in Crossmolina, about eight miles away.

The Collins family had already suffered tragedy in their lives. Bridie and Sandra's only brother, James, then 27, was killed in an accident in the factory where he worked. His mother, Eleanor, was devastated. She had lost her husband when the children were very small, Bridie was only three at the time. Eleanor had since remarried and James lived with them and was very close to his mother and stepfather. James died just six months before Sandra disappeared. Now of the three siblings, only Bridie is left.

There were happy moments too, of course. Bridie's wedding was a high point for the family. She got married while James was alive and before Sandra disappeared, but neither of them ever met Michelle, Bridie's vivacious daughter, now 18 months old.

Sandra's disappearance wasn't reported until the following day when her aunt Ann rang Bridie to say she hadn't returned home the previous night. Bridie wasn't worried at the time, Sandra was 29 years of age and could have gone to visit friends for the evening and stayed overnight. The only strange thing as far as she could see was that Sandra never stayed away without letting somebody know where she was.

Bridie tried to think of any reason why Sandra wouldn't have phoned her aunt. The two were good friends but she wondered had they had a row or some kind of a falling out and could Sandra have stayed away without phoning Ann as a result of that.

Bridie said to wait for a while and to phone her later if Sandra didn't turn up. However, Bridie says she was quite confident her sister would return home, that she had probably stayed with friends for some reason and that Ann was worrying about nothing. She kept reminding herself that Sandra was 29 years old and perfectly entitled to stay out if she wanted to.

After work, Bridie checked with Ann but there had been no sign of Sandra. This was getting serious. She then drove to Killala where she walked around the town and spoke to her sister's friends, asking if they'd seen her, but nobody had. Bridie then raised the alarm with the local Gardaí and they took over the search. There was no indication that Sandra had planned to go anywhere. They checked her room and all her clothes and personal possessions were there.

Bridie says that for the first couple of months there was great searching but that has died down now.

The Collins family are convinced that something happened to Sandra in the town of Killala itself and that somebody locally has information that could lead to the recovery of her body. They are quite certain that she is dead, that she was killed that night.

A few days later Sandra's jacket was found at the pier in the harbour, in the pocket was the packet of sausages she had bought earlier in the local shop.

Following her disappearance the Gardaí organised searches of the area for three Sundays in a row. 'Loads of people turned up', says Bridie, 'they were very good, they searched miles and miles of fields and sub aqua divers searched the area around the pier. But there was no trace of her, nothing.'

The family are agreed that she was the victim of foul play, but why won't anyone come forward with the information that could give the family some closure, some comfort? 'Did somebody see something and they're covering up for someone else?' asks Bridie. She finds it hard to accept that in a town the size of Killala someone could abduct a young woman and possibly murder her without anyone noticing. It's a town where people know the local cars and who is driving what and who is out and about late at night.

Every month or so Bridie talks to the gardaí in Killala and they tell her about any updates in the investigation. Gardaí walk the shoreline regularly. Sandra's mum and stepfather, Joe, go back to Killala often and search for her. Bridie finds it too hard, 'I only go an odd time, I get too upset and then I come back and I'm filled with anger knowing there is someone down there who knows something and who won't come forward. It's very hard on my mum. I used to think it was just as hard for me until I gave birth to my own little girl. I don't know how my mother gets on with her life at all.'

Bridie says that every day they are hoping she will turn up but 'if the news is bad, we want to know that too. If we could bring home her body, at least we'd have a grave to go to.' They already have one grave to go to – that of her brother James. On his anniversary, on his birthday and at Christmas, they visit his grave and bring flowers 'but for Sandra, there is nothing'.

'In the meantime we light candles for her and hope she'll make contact with us some day. You'd hate to think that people would forget her or the other missing people.'

10

Pearse Cremin

'200 Heineken trucks left the city with his face on the side.'

Born 30 July, 1972.
Missing from Cork City since 31 October, 2000.

The Cremin family once again found it particularly hard when the Cork Jazz festival kicked off last October. The annual bank holiday weekend that most people think of in terms of fun, music and craic forced the Cremin family to once again relive the nightmare they experienced when their beloved son, Pearse, went missing in the aftermath of the festival three years ago.

Pearse had lived it up over the weekend of the jazz festival in October 2000, heading out with friends on the Friday evening and staying away until the Sunday evening. He was living with his brother

Cormac at the time and gave him a shout on his way home on the Sunday to see if anyone in the house wanted a take-away. Cormac jumped at the offer of a burger and chips and got beers out from the fridge. When Pearse arrived, himself, Cormac and his family had an enjoyable evening, laughing and joking and chatting. That was the last such evening they would enjoy together before Pearse vanished.

Cormac had been delighted to offer Pearse, his younger brother and best friend, a room in his house when rents went up in October and Pearse and his flatmates decided they would give notice on their apartment and await a fall in rent before finding somewhere else. Pearse had been staying with Cormac for two weeks when he went missing. Cormac and his wife Bernadette had turned the playroom into a bedroom for him, and Cormac's son, Tadgh, was thrilled to have the company of his uncle and godfather, whom he adored.

On the Tuesday, 31 October, the last day Pearse was seen, he went to work as normal. He was a tennis coach and, together with a friend, ran his own business, supplying tennis courses to schools throughout Cork. Pearse adored tennis and this was the second year of a career that he thoroughly enjoyed. He had countless trophies which he had received over the years for his successes in the sport. On the Tuesday, Pearse had lunch with a friend and colleague and after work the two met up again. Pearse didn't come back to his brother's house that evening, which was certainly not a cause for concern. He was 27 years old, had his own key and there was nothing strange about him choosing to stay overnight with a friend.

It wasn't until the following day, Wednesday, that anyone noticed Pearse was missing. His friend called around to the house that evening looking for him. He said he was supposed to meet up with him that evening and wondered whether he was around. Cormac, unconcerned, invited the friend to wait and called a couple of Pearse's friends to see if he was with them. But as Cormac began to phone more and more people, who had heard nothing from Pearse, he began to get worried. At ten o'clock that evening Cormac rang his parents and other family members to see if they had heard from Pearse.

Cormac thought it was quite strange that none of the 30 or so people he rang had heard anything from his younger brother. It was unusual that Pearse wouldn't have made contact with any of them. It then emerged that he hadn't turned up to work that morning. Cormac decided to let it lie for the evening, guessing that Pearse was probably out somewhere in the aftermath of the jazz festival weekend. He was young, good looking and single after all. Though he was a little worried, Cormac decided not to overreact. At the end of the day, Pearse was his own person, and was entitled to do his own thing, though it was very out of character for him not to turn up to work without letting anybody know.

The next day, when there was no sign of Pearse or no report of anyone having seen him, the family were very concerned and they declared him missing at teatime.

The last time he had been seen was when he left his friend's house on the Tuesday evening. It emerged that the two had set out in separate cars and, on the Southlink Road, Pearse turned left, apparently to go home to Cormac's house.

On Friday morning, the family launched a full-scale search. A massive crowd gathered, including family, friends, colleagues and members of the two soccer teams Pearse played for. They searched everywhere, all over Cork City and Cork County. They got fliers out to CIE, which were put in all the buses in Cork. Huge posters were also put on 200 Heineken trucks leaving the county. A friend of Cormac's worked in Heineken and offered to put the posters up as it would expose his picture to thousands of people who might take note and remember seeing him somewhere.

The search party was massive. Pearse was one of six children and a hugely popular figure in Cork City, a member of two soccer teams, one of which Cormac also played for. Everyone gathered round to assist the Cremin family but a week passed and fear of what could have happened to Pearse increased. The search went on night and day, week after week. The intensive, non-stop search was conducted by up to 30 people every night for about three months, but to no avail.

There was a positive sighting of Pearse in a garage 10 days after he went missing by an old school friend of his. He bumped into Pearse in the garage and, not having seen him for a long time, he had a quick chat with him, not realising that Pearse was missing. He immediately reported the sighting when he saw the posters. However, by the time the family found out and looked for the video tapes from the garage for the time in question, they had been taped over.

There were endless other calls about sightings, only to end in heartbreak when they led to nothing. The family was lucky to have such a large crew searching for Pearse, but often people would mistake someone else for him. His picture was in the local paper every day and the local radio station was a huge help, doing interviews with the family and reading out announcements.

No one could understand where Pearse had got to. There were no signs at all that he had been planning to go away. He hadn't taken any extra clothes with him, nor had he taken a passport. He had never travelled before. He had his wallet with him, but his bank account wasn't touched and didn't show up as having been used in the English banking system either.

The family was distraught and bewildered at the complete blank they were drawing. It wasn't in Pearse's nature to do something like this. He was very close to his family, a real home bird, typically up at his parents' home most Tuesdays and Thursdays for dinner. He and Cormac were incredibly close and Cormac just couldn't understand where he had got to. Cormac knew Pearse really well, they shared all their worries with each other, and Cormac was literally flabbergasted at the thought that Pearse could have taken off of his own accord without saying anything to him.

'The two of us were best friends. We were always very close. Pearse is 10 years younger than me. I was in the Navy for nine years and I remember when I came back he'd grown up and the relationship of older and younger brother became that of best friends.' The two were very similar and had a huge amount in common. They were both soccer addicts, playing for the Cork Business League team. Pearse, a great athlete, also played for another team, as well as pursuing his passion for tennis. The house was full of trophies that Pearse had won for tennis achievements. 'Pearse loved tennis and he always practised. No matter what he'd do, he'd be good at it.'

What really puzzles Cormac is that his brother always told him everything. They shared all their secrets and he hadn't noticed any signs that something was bothering Pearse in the run up to his disappearance. He knew Pearse so well, and would have thought that he would have been the first to realise if there was something wrong. Pearse wasn't the type to worry. He was such a happy person, always great fun, always the one to suggest an impromptu night out for a few beers and a bit of craic. It was always Pearse who would instigate the nights that would start out as one drink in a pub and hours later everyone would still be out, after a great evening, filled with laughter and fun.

At 27 years of age, Pearse was a typical lad. He had girlfriends on and off but never anything too serious. Being a good-looking guy, he was never short of female admirers. He had loads of friends and was dedicated to his job to the extent that he would never go out to the pub any night before he was due to teach tennis to children at weekends. He would never smoke in front of the children he instructed. The situation was a mystery.

Apart from the positive sighting in the garage, the last time Pearse was seen was when he was driving his blue Fiat Brava away from his friend's house that night. A car does not disappear as easily as a person and Cormac felt from the first moment that Pearse's car would be the key to discovering what happened to Pearse. 'I thought if we found the blue Fiat Brava, we'd find him.' The search for the car wore on for three months. Once again, there were sightings of it all over, however they all led to a dead end. There were countless blue Fiat Bravas on the road.

Cormac had a feeling about the mobile home he owned in Robert's Cove, outside Cork. Pearse had a key for the place. He'd been out there with his friends the weekend of the jazz festival. Cormac thought if Pearse wanted to get away for a while, that would be the logical place for him to go and he kept going back to Robert's Cove to look for him. Sergeant John Deasy from Cork station had a gut feeling about Robert's Cove as well and he went along with Cormac to search. The day they went it was quite foggy and the sergeant said they would come back with Garda divers.

Cormac worked just three miles from Robert's Cove and was continually drawn back. One day, about three and a half months after Pearse went missing, he was standing on the top of the cliff looking out over the sea when he spotted the number plate of Pearse's car. He immediately telephoned Sergeant Deasy and the Gardaí came out. They found glass at the edge of the cliff where the car must have gone over. Cormac and one of Pearse's friends went down and found more fragments of glass and the number plate. The glass was sent off for analysis and the tests returned positive, the glass was from a Fiat Brava car. The divers went down and the car was found. It was Pearse's car.

There was no evidence that Pearse had been in the car. The divers brought it into shallow water. The next morning Cormac went down to the car. 'I was saying to myself "don't let there be a body part in there", but in another way I wanted there to be a body, so that we could give him a burial.'

The gardaí actually had to ask what type of car it was because it was such a wreck. The roof and doors were gone. They can't know whether or not Pearse had been in the car but certain signs indicated that he had not been. There was no sign of a key, the seatbelt wasn't fastened and the divers didn't recover a body.

Cormac says that the divers will probably go back and dive again. The longer the search in the water goes on the more Cormac wonders if Pearse is there at all. He believes that Pearse is alive, but he is very confused as to where his brother could be. He is particularly upset to think that Pearse may have had something on his mind that he felt he couldn't share with him, as Cormac says no problem would have been too big to solve. The very fact that Pearse felt so comfortable staying with Cormac and his family was surely testament to the fact that he knew they were there for him, that they would do anything for him.

'My gut feeling is that he's alive. I just don't understand it though. I knew him very well. He would tell me everything, all his personal stuff. If he had problems, they could have been sorted; that's why he was here with us – we loved him. He knew he didn't even have to ask, he wouldn't have moved in if he didn't, that's the way we operated. Pearse never went missing before. When he stayed with a friend, he'd arrive in the following morning, saying "I stayed in blah's last night, we ended up in…".'

Cormac says the upsetting thing is that, unknown to his family, something may have been bothering Pearse. 'There were no signs, that's a killer. In general Pearse seemed in good form. There was nothing that would have driven him to do something stupid.'

'I've spoken to people since who went missing themselves or have contemplated going missing. People rang me to see if I wanted to talk to them and I've met up with them and they've told me what it's like from their perspective.'

After the car was found, the search drew a complete blank, which Cormac says is a total disaster. 'I went up to my mother and said we've got good news, we've found the car and he wasn't in it. In my heart I knew it wasn't alright though, because the car was the key. As the guards put it, all possible angles were exhausted.'

Pearse's family would try anything that they believed might lead to finding Pearse. Two psychics also worked on the case, one of them was of no help, while the other was often quite accurate. Cormac sought the latter out himself, after hearing about him through friends: 'He felt Pearse was dead, in water, before the car was found. He didn't locate him but the things he did say were incredible. We spent days in boats dragging and searching areas that he got a feeling about.'

Although the second psychic didn't locate Pearse, Cormac says he was very genuine, that he hadn't made any promises and was just doing his best to help. Also, he hadn't approached them and he wouldn't even take money for his work. 'His method was very precise and once he pinpointed a specific house, another time a spot on a river.' The family investigated the areas pinpointed, but nothing turned up.

Through his experience of searching for Pearse, Cormac has become very involved in working for families of missing people in Ireland. He can understand and identify acutely with what they are going through, and his experience can often be a great help to families who don't know where to start when a loved one disappears.

Cormac has become very involved in setting up a formal structure to assist families of people who have gone missing. He says it is very difficult to know what to do when someone goes missing just like that, nobody expects it and they don't know what to do. 'When Pearse went missing, I picked up the Golden Pages to see if there was a Missing Persons Helpline. I rang the number listed for three days, it was constantly engaged. I discovered that it hadn't been manned for two years. I asked why it was still in the book. Apparently some magazine in Dublin sponsored it, but, two years later, they were not sponsoring it anymore and if anyone rang it they just got an engaged tone.' This is just a further waste of time for people who are fighting against time as it is.

When Thomas Linehan went missing in Cork just after the Christmas following Pearse's disappearance, Cormac rang his son, David, and said that he had a team of people already out looking for Pearse in South Cork, so he could concentrate on the North side. 'I asked him for a poster of his father and we did up 500 copies and distributed them.' Sadly, David Linehan found his father's remains washed up three months later.

Following this contact, Cormac and David both agreed that there was little or nothing in place to assist people in finding someone who has gone missing, especially at the crucial moment when they could most do with the assistance. The two decided they would set something up as soon as possible. They got together and began their work by setting up a Missing Persons Helpline in Cork, so that families have somewhere to turn to immediately when someone goes missing.

'We plagued Minister O'Donoghue for two years to get him to set up a national helpline. We sent him about 10,000 letters. He wouldn't do it. He had spoken to Mary Phelan and promised the first thing he'd do when he was in office was set up a helpline. Eventually Michael McDowell TD set it up two weeks before the general election.'

Cormac and David continued raising funds and carrying out work to assist families of missing people. When another person went missing in the area, they spent three weeks looking for him, taking only Christmas day off. Cormac remembers how the man's family waited on the quayside, while the Gardaí, the Navy and divers organised by Cormac and David searched the water. Eventually a ship picked the car and body up on sonar eight weeks later. The family were extremely grateful for the huge assistance they received from Cormac, David and their team at a time when they most needed it. 'The family wanted to give us money. We wouldn't let them so they had a fundraiser and raised €9,800.' Cormac and David bought a boat with the proceeds, which they can send out immediately if there is an alert in the area. Recently they also bought a search and rescue dog, which they are training to assist in future searches.

Cormac and David believe there is a serious lack of resources when it comes to launching a search for missing people. There is only one Garda sub aqua team and that is based in Dublin, which means they may have a few hours journey before they even begin to dive for a body. Cormac thinks there should be a sub aqua team in all the main cities for the sole purpose of diving for missing people. 'The Garda sub aqua team is based in Dublin. They'll only come down if they are pretty certain there is a body in there. They'll search for one day and then leave. You can only call the Navy in after the Guards have gone.'

When they came down to look for Pearse, the Garda sub aqua team didn't even get out of the boat as it was too rough. Cormac isn't blaming the Gardaí for this. 'It's not their fault. They don't have the resources or the training. There should be a Garda sub aqua team in all the main cities, so if someone goes missing, they can react immediately, instead you could be waiting for months for them.'

The disappearance of their 27-year-old son has had a devastating effect on Pearse's parents. His mother, Monica, who is now 62, had a stroke two months after he went missing. Both she and Pearse's father, Denis, have been under tremendous strain. 'Pearse was very close to Mum. It's breaking my parents' hearts.' Pearse's parents were very upset recently when they were asked to give DNA samples to keep on file 'just in case'. The effect on the parents is always acute – the worst nightmare for any father or mother is to see anything happen to the child they created, nurtured and watched growing up.

There was also a huge strain on Cormac's family life. He had two small children when Pearse went missing, but was constantly out conducting the search. It was very difficult for Bernadette and the children, who gave him huge support. Cormac was also extremely fortunate in work as they gave him a lot of slack and facilitated him by giving him time off. 'I am a lucky guy. I work for a very good friend. I was out all night most nights. Luckily I had a mobile phone, so I could work and do the search at night.'

The fact that a member of someone's family has gone missing doesn't mean that the rest of the world stops until they are found. The brutal reality is that life continues. Companies cannot come to a standstill because one of their employees is looking for a missing member of their family, and without work, there is no income, hence no bread on the table. It is a vicious circle to have to face the extra stresses when one is already completely consumed by the disappearance of a family member. This is the reality that people are faced with.

Pearse's siblings, Seán, Donnchadh, Cormac, Pádraig and Siobhán, are all finding it very difficult to deal with his disappearance. Cormac got severely depressed, and was unable to sleep at night. In the end he had to go to his doctor who prescribed sleeping tablets to allow him to get some rest. The family were driven mad by Pearse's disappearance. It was very difficult not to lose control altogether. 'I nearly went off the rails, I think we all nearly lost it', says Cormac.

It gets to the stage when families of missing people will try anything if they think it holds any hope of locating their missing family member. 'This woman from the States made contact with us through the website. She said she was a visionary and that she was working on two cases about missing Irish people. She pinpointed Pearse to a place in West Cork six months ago – giving us a description of a place with a lighthouse in front and an island behind. We e-mailed her a map and she pinpointed the location in West Cork. She said that Pearse was terminally ill. We came upon a "centre" out in the middle of nowhere, two miles up the road from where she'd said he'd be, a place we found on the Internet under a search for places where people who were ill would be. We spent three days out there sussing it out. The people there wouldn't give us any details of who stayed there. They said they kept no records, that it was a place of well-being.'

Cormac was convinced Pearse was there and sneaked in over the fence one night. He showed a picture of Pearse to a 'hippy' type staying there, who said he hadn't seen him. Cormac found the place extremely eerie and very strange. After a few days hanging around the centre and having eventually gaining entry he no longer thinks he is there.

The search for Pearse continues. The hardest times for the family are understandably Pearse's birthday, Christmas and the arrival of the Cork Jazz Festival every year, bringing with it another anniversary of Pearse's mysterious disappearance. Cormac is heartbroken not knowing where his younger brother is or what happened to him.

There is a photo in the family's sitting room of Pearse holding Cormac's youngest son Neil in his arms when he was a baby. Neil is now three and doesn't remember his uncle. Cormac's other son, Tadgh, is Pearse's godson, and says a prayer for his godfather every night. Though he is only seven, he understands that his father is suffering a lot and always asks him how the search for Pearse is going and how his father is feeling.

Meanwhile Cormac gets through the day by stepping out the door and holding his head up high. 'I deal with it by searching for other people and continuing to follow all leads to Pearse. I do believe he is still alive.'

11

Aengus Shanahan

'If you're out there Aengus, please come home, just for a little while.'

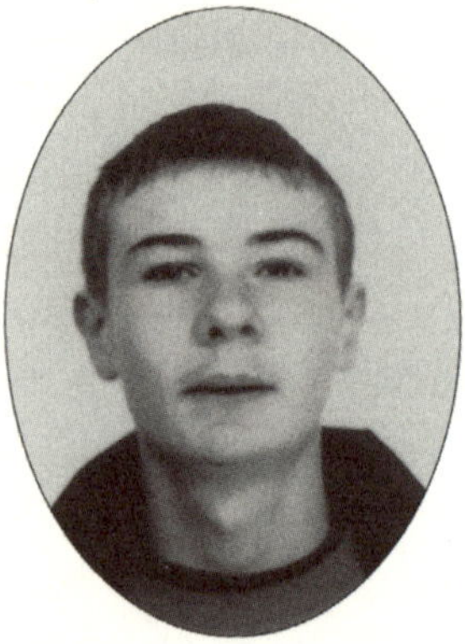

Born 23 January, 1980.
Missing from Limerick City since 11 February, 2000.

There is a laneway in Limerick City known as 'Angela's Ashes Lane' and that was the scene of the last reported sighting of 20-year-old Aengus 'Gussie' Shanahan, who disappeared in February 2000.

Aengus is the baby in the Shanahan family. His sister, Reiltin, is the eldest, followed by Gráinne and his brother, Roibeard. The Shanahans are a typical example of a family that has been devastated by the loss of their youngest child. It changes perspectives, it becomes the main topic of conversation, even when they are not talking about it, it's always there, hovering like a cloud over the family.

At the time Aengus disappeared, his father, Bob Shanahan, was the manager of the Bank of Ireland in O'Connell Street. He has now retired but remembers well the afternoon in February 2000 when Aengus called in to see him, as was usual on a Friday, to cash his pay cheque.

That day Aengus called in and told his dad that he was going out that evening with a few friends. Aengus was meticulous in planning a night out and didn't leave anything to chance. He was planning to stay out so he had already arranged a bed for the night with friends in the city. This was typical of Aengus, an organised young man with close contact with family and friends.

Bob recalls the last day he saw Aengus: 'I met him about twenty past three. He came into the office to me; he told me he was going out to meet a few pals and would be having a few scoops beforehand.'

After Aengus left his dad, he went across the road to Supermacs to use the phone there to ring his friends and to make the arrangements for the evening. We have to remember that three years ago it wasn't the norm for everyone to have a mobile phone and young people were far more dependent on pay phones. Following his son's disappearance, Supermacs very kindly allowed Bob to view their camera footage. The video clearly shows Aengus meeting his friend some time after he made the phone call.

The friends then went on to Coopers Bar, which is just across the road from the flat where Aengus was planning to stay the night. Bob had no reason to worry about Aengus going out, he was 20 years old, older than many of the young people out on the town that Friday evening.

Later in the evening the friends split up. Aengus said he wanted to go on to a disco, the others – a boy and a girl – decided they wanted to stay on in Coopers. Aengus decided to leave and go to the disco anyway, a few minutes walk away. Again, the CCTV cameras picked Aengus up as he left the bar on his own. He stood for a while in the doorway of the pub and chatted to the bouncers and with a small group of people who were standing around. All of the people who showed up on the video have been identified by the Gardaí and interviewed, but they were unable to throw any further light on what happened to Aengus after he left the pub.

Aengus then walked across the road in the rain with a bottle of beer in his hand. As he crossed the road, he almost walked into a car that had been parked in front of Coopers. It transpired that the woman motorist in the car lived just a few doors away from the pub and was stopped there, waiting for a parking space near her home to become free so that she could get out quickly in the morning for work. This was normal, just one of the problems encountered by motorists who live in a city. At the same time that a parking space became free, Aengus walked across the road, so the woman in the car noticed him. She says she saw him go down the laneway, a shortcut to the disco, and that was the last definite sighting of him, nothing has been seen of him since.

Since then the family say they haven't heard one iota. 'We have an open mind about it', says Bob Shanahan.

Nevertheless, the family has been very hurt in recent months by an article in a Sunday newspaper. The article claimed that Aengus had been captured by a drugs gang and murdered and that his body simply hasn't been found. Bob wrote to the editor of the paper and asked for his letter to be published, a letter which pointed out that there was no known connection between Aengus and any drugs gang, but the letter was never published. Bob says that although he was not afforded a right of reply, there was no point in taking the matter any further, the paper wasn't taking him and his concerns seriously at all. 'You only make it worse', he says.

However, he was upset by the fact that people who didn't know the family saw the article about Aengus in the paper and might have thought that Aengus was mixed up in the drugs scene in some way. The Shanahans are practical people and acknowledge that although they haven't uncovered any negative things about their son's life, no one knows what the final answer may be. Until Aengus is found, no one can know exactly what happened to him.

The family is also aware that they might not like something they learn about their son's disappearance. 'As long as we find him, that's the main thing. We mightn't like what we find but, if he came back with problems, we'd have to handle it. We'd help him out no matter what', says Bob.

But, as a family, the Shanahans had been well checked out by both the Gardaí and the FBI. This happened prior to the September 1998 visit to Ireland of President Bill Clinton and his wife, Hillary. The location for the President's Limerick speech was O'Connell Street, right outside the Bank of Ireland branch where Bob was manager. The bank building itself was to be used for dignitaries to meet the Presidential party and for guests to get ready before the event. Because of this, extensive Garda and FBI checks were carried out on all bank officials and their families. As manager, Bob's family was included in that security check. There were no negative results, no problem in having Bob so close to the Presidential party. Bob is very pleased about this because he now has the certainty that the checks on his family didn't throw up anything strange about Aengus. He believes that had his son had contact with any questionable characters, then this would have been brought to light at that stage. Also, in his role as a bank manager, Bob would be well known to Gardaí.

And there was something else – senior gardaí told Bob that his son's name had never arisen when they were questioning known drug dealers over the years. 'I've had a lot of transactions with the Gardaí over the years', says Bob, 'and they tell me that in all their dealings with drug dealers in the Limerick area, not one of them ever mentioned any connection with Aengus. Usually, they told me, you would get a whisper of something.'

Bob says the family is happy with the way the Gardaí have handled the search for Aengus. They have supplemented this with their own search but it's very difficult they say because, 'when someone goes missing like this, you haven't a clue where to start'. The family has been joined in the search by friends, neighbours and colleagues from the bank.

The Bank of Ireland also agreed to put up posters of Aengus alongside their PASS machines. Bob figured that so many people, Aengus included, use ATM machines, that someone might recognise him, might remember something. Unfortunately nothing positive has come from that.

On the Monday morning, Bob set about investigating his son's account at the bank, to see if he had made a large withdrawal and possibly moved away from Limerick. The bank can tell exactly which PASS machine is used to withdraw money but there was no information there on Aengus.

'On Monday morning when I went to the bank I checked his account. He used his bank card on a regular basis, he's a "dipper", he'd take out 20 here and 20 there as he needed it. But when I checked his account, nothing had been taken out.'

When Aengus disappeared, he had about 90 pounds on him. A friend paid back a loan to him but he in turn had paid his father some money he owed him. His account has been monitored ever since his disappearance and neither his PASS card nor account have been used. Aengus was sensible about money, when he got paid every fortnight, he put aside a certain amount for his investments. By the following week he might be broke and getting a 'sub' from his Dad, but he always returned whatever he had borrowed.

Aengus was generous with his family and insisted on paying for the re-vamping of his own bedroom. He installed a special timber floor and decorated his room the way he wanted it. Bob sees this as further evidence that Aengus wasn't planning to go anywhere.

There is now a new poster which the family has distributed around Irish pubs in England and Scotland. They say they want Aengus to contact them because of ill health in the family and there has been considerable ill health since Aengus disappeared. His mother, Nancy, a retired teacher, suffered a stroke in May 2001. The Shanahans had been planning to go abroad on holiday when Nancy collapsed and was found on the landing of their home. She has made a good recovery but now needs the aid of a wheelchair and a walking frame to get around. In recent weeks Bob broke both his legs when he fell from a ladder. He is making a good recovery but has both legs in plaster. Between himself and Nancy he said their home was like the television programme *ER* for a time. They relied very much on the goodwill of their other children to keep going.

Aengus' sisters and brother also suffered from the disappearance of their brother although they would say the whole family is very strong and very positive. 'But there are times when you are going to be down and you are always hoping that you will get some break, that some new information will emerge', says Bob, 'we're always hoping he's alive, but we just don't know'.

Because Aengus was staying overnight with a friend, Bob and his wife Nancy didn't realise that their son was missing until the Sunday evening when he didn't return home. If someone else was involved in his disappearance this gave them time to abduct Aengus, to cover their tracks or even to hide the body.

Aengus was due in work at four o'clock on Monday afternoon so his parents decided to wait and see if he turned up for work. 'At a quarter past four he hadn't turned up and we began to get really worried'. The Shanahans raised the alarm with the Gardaí and the search began.

Fr Aquinas Duffy is a nephew of Nancy's. When there was no sign of his cousin returning home, he searched the web to find a suitable site for missing persons where he could set up his cousin's details and leave a message for him. He couldn't find anything, so he decided to start his own website (see Chapter 3). This has now grown into Ireland's Missing Persons website. Working from his presbytery in Tallaght originally and now from Bray in Co. Wicklow, the website has grown and carries updates and messages dealing with all the missing people in Ireland and some from abroad who were missing while visiting this country.

Bob and Nancy are delighted with the website. 'You can get around the world with it, you know that people in the most remote places can check it and see his picture and know that he's missing. It's an ongoing thing and that's great because sometimes nothing is moving and you feel so frustrated. The website helps a lot.'

In common with most families who have lost a loved one, the Shanahans have sought the assistance of psychics. It is hard to choose a psychic because you have to rely on the advice of friends, on the recommendation of people who have used them before you. Sometimes psychics contact the family and give them hair-raising information which upsets everyone and which rarely pinpoints the missing person. Bob is now very sceptical of the advice given by the psychics he consulted, he said their contradictory advice 'would nearly drive you cuckoo'. They sent the family all over the country, to Glenflesk in Kerry, to Feakle in Co. Clare and to Dublin. They found out that the only thing one of these psychics had ever found was a dog! Then there was one in the US who told them their son had been taken away in a van by people with dogs. 'These fellows are a bloody nuisance', says Bob, 'but the very minute somebody is found or a body is discovered, they try to claim the credit for it'.

Bob and Nancy are totally perplexed by their son's disappearance. They still spend a great deal of their time going over and over the last days he was at home with them and trying to remember any clues, any differences in him that might explain something. They have spoken to his friends who have been very co-operative but they are no closer to the truth.

'We have been in touch with the Gardaí constantly, they have nothing, they haven't got one clue', says Bob. He himself puts forward two possible scenarios: 'Either one of two things happened – because you just couldn't disappear from a laneway in the middle of the night – either he met somebody he knew and got in and went away with them or else he was actually dragged into a car.' Nobody saw this happen and there were no cameras to record him either getting into a car with someone he knew or being abducted against his will. But whatever did happen, it was all over in a matter of minutes, in the space of time before anybody else walked down 'Angela's Ashes' laneway.

Bob believes Aengus is still alive: 'He didn't seem to plan to be going away. Whenever he went away on holidays before, he would always pack well in advance. He didn't go away that often and he'd always tell us beforehand. He'd plan it, he'd have his little case. He was very tidy. I'm hoping he is still alive.'

Following appeals for information, there were a number of reported sightings of Aengus in England, and particularly in London. Bob decided to travel over and spend some time going around the places where homeless people might hang out. Over a few days they covered enormous distances and visited hostels and feedings centres, speaking to young people who came from Ireland, who could have known Aengus and hoping against hope that they might actually find Aengus and bring him home.

'My son and I went to London last year and we spent a bit of time there and we checked out a lot of places, the centres all round Piccadilly, the homeless places all round.' But they found no trace of Aengus. However, Bob believes that many of the homeless protect one another when someone comes around asking questions. The theory is that the homeless are always delighted when someone comes looking for them, that they want to come home and would be glad to be found. But, says Bob, 'one of the things you find in London among the homeless is that some may want to be found but they protect one another from prying eyes and when you go round asking questions, most of them will close up and won't give you any information'.

Back in Limerick the Shanahans are convinced there is definitely somebody who knows what happened to Aengus, 'a hole didn't just open up in that laneway. Somebody actually does know what happened.'

Then there is the question of conscience. Nancy says she is certain that somebody in Limerick itself knows what happened to her son. She appeals to their conscience and the possibility of an anonymous tip off, 'they don't even have to come to us, just get a message to us', she says. She has already considered how they could do this, through the Garda confidential line, other Garda phone numbers, a priest or even in the confessional.

The family has always appealed just for the information, 'to let us know that he's alright, that he's alive. We don't know if he's dead or alive. He's entitled to go missing, we would respect that if he wanted to stay away. He wouldn't be the first person that went away, if we just knew that Aengus is okay.'

And if the news is bad? They would still want to know. 'Well I reared Aengus up to 20 years of age and we're not going to give in without a battle. We'll always be here for him', says Bob.

Nancy believes that her son was abducted against his will. She still concentrates on the belief that 'somebody knows something, somebody saw something, he didn't disappear off the face of the earth'. Of course, they have considered every possibility, abduction, kidnapping, even murder; the problem is there is no evidence to prove anything.

And if Aengus could hear her, if someone could get a message to him for her, this is what Nancy wants him to hear, 'please come back Aengus. And if you want to stay away, you're welcome, but we'll welcome you back, just for a little while.'

12

Ellen Coss

(née Brown)

'Did she ever get on the boat?'

Born 30 April, 1949.
Missing from Holyhead since 3 November, 1999.

Ellen Coss disappeared on 3 November, 1999, in Holyhead while returning to Dublin from Manchester where she had recently visited her sister, Bertha Lee, née Brown. Ellen had been married but was separated for many years. She has an adult son, Peter, now aged 30 and living in London, who according to family and friends was 'the light of her life'.

Before she went missing, Ellen suffered from depression and had received help from both AWARE and Gingerbread, but her family has ruled out suicide as a possible reason for her disappearance. She didn't smoke or drink but loved walking and traditional Irish music. She was best known to her neighbours in Milltown as a community worker. She even arranged for RTÉ's 'Dustin' to attend a fundraising event in the neighbourhood. Her friend Rosemary Martin remembers that 'she got things done, she was tough'. But in the end 'she became disenchanted and disillusioned'.

Ellen Coss would now be 53 years old. She grew up in Ballyfermot in Dublin but had lived in Windy Arbour for the nine years before she disappeared. She has three brothers, Tom, Roy and James William and one sister, Bertha.

On the day she went missing she said goodbye to the sister she adored and got on the train. She had only about 10 pounds on her. Rosemary says there is something that she feels hasn't been fully investigated. 'When Ellen got on the train, her sister got on with her to see her off. Ellen sat beside a man. She is a chatty person and must have got into conversation with him.' That's all they know, but a psychic told the family she had been murdered so they continue to wonder about this man on the train.

From there on, the picture fades. No one knows if she did actually catch the Holyhead boat because on that date, the CCTV wasn't working and there are no tapes to check.

It was two days before anyone realised that she was missing. Her brother, Tom, searched for her for days, trying to piece together some idea of what could have happened to her. Where was she last seen? Did she ever get on the boat?

The family talk of the trauma they suffer when a body is reported washed up on a beach somewhere. Last March, the body of one poor woman was washed up near the south coast of England at Eastbourne. Police in England started trawling through a missing person's list and by June believed it might be Ellen as it seemed a close match. Her sister, Bertha, actually travelled from Manchester to view the remains. Having been told of some identifying marks, she was certain it was her sister but was told the body could not be released by the coroner until the results of DNA tests were known.

A backlog in testing at UK laboratories meant the family had to wait six months until the results of the DNA tests came through. 'We spent six months hoping we had found her', says Tom, 'but the tests proved it wasn't her'. He said the wait was a heartbreaking experience for the whole family. 'I have become ill because of it', he says, 'and it is hitting Bertha very hard. We kept thinking she would ring and we would give her time to get herself together but the waiting was awful. Ellen was like a mother to me. We were inseparable and now as a family we are going through torture.'

They tried to think of all the little things which might help to identify their sister, like the one silver earring she always wore or her magnificent teeth. However, the fact that she hadn't been to a dentist in nine years meant she had no dental records. They were destroyed as part of routine dental surgery procedure when she hadn't attended for so long.

Tom says 'there was a certain amount of relief when we knew it wasn't Ellen, but then the whole thing starts up again. If it's not her, what did happen to her?'

The family of another missing woman, Rita Roche from north Dublin, went through a remarkably similar experience to the Browns, but, in their case, a body washed up on Christmas Eve 2000 *did* prove to be that of the 45-year-old Dubliner. Rita is thought to have fallen into the River Tolka on a stormy night a month earlier and her body washed into Dublin Bay before being somehow swept the 200 miles to the west coast of Scotland. It took four months before her body was finally identified through DNA tests.

Ellen's family put up posters in shop windows all over south Dublin, hoping someone might have seen her, might recognise her. Tom and Bertha believe Ellen will come back some day. 'Sometimes I feel Ellen around me', Tom says, 'I can feel her laughing'. Their message to Ellen remains the same as it always has been: 'Please get in touch and let us know you are safe and well. Your well-being is all that matters to the family. We love and miss you so much Ellen.'

Tom says his sister is a wonderful person. 'She did everything, she was a childminder, a hairdresser. She was a great one for community work. My fondest memory of her is when Pope John Paul II was in Ireland in 1979 and Ellen handed him a rose. This is all so hard.'

13

Seán Ryan

He packed a bag and set off on his travels.

Born 29 June, 1981.
Missing from Downpatrick, Co. Down since 2 September, 1998.

Seán left home of his own accord, didn't say anything about the fact that he was leaving, but met at least two people over the following week who didn't suspect anything was the matter.

The 17-year-old lived in Downpatrick in Co. Down and was studying for his A levels. It was the first day of term and Seán was due back at school to begin his final year's study, but he had no intention of being there. This, of course, we only know in hindsight.

It was a normal morning in the Ryan household. Seán's mum and dad, Gerry and Patricia, were up and about early, getting ready for work. They didn't disturb him before they left but they had spoken to him the night before. They didn't notice anything unusual; there was nothing about their son to alarm them. He talked about school and study and seemed to be relaxed and looking forward to getting on with his studies.

However, Seán didn't go to school that day. Instead, he packed a bag and set off on his travels, a journey that would just a few days later swallow him up as he joined the ranks of the disappeared.

That evening, Gerry and Patricia came home from work but there was no sign of Seán. They waited a while, thinking he had something on after school hours, but then reasoned that it was only the first day of term and too early to have any extras on his timetable. They considered all possibilities, maybe he had stayed on to study, maybe he had gone to work at his part-time job, but they became increasingly anxious when he didn't arrive home.

Seán is the second youngest in a family of five children. His parents say he always contacted home if he was delayed or if he had to work late. He was interested in catering and had a part-time job in the local hotel which he seemed to enjoy.

Eventually, Gerry and Patricia decided to phone around Seán's friends to see if he had gone somewhere after school or if there was some event on that day he had forgotten to tell them about. But no one had seen him, there were no plans to do anything after school and his parents learned the worst news of all, he hadn't even been to school.

The Ryans have since learned something of what Seán did that day. Instead of going to school, he headed for Belfast. It was very much a planned, if secret, trip. He had packed a bag with his clothes and had taken £300 from his savings. He took the bus to Belfast and, in what was to be the first of a number of coincidences, he bumped into someone he knew in the city, an acquaintance he knew from school. Later this young man said that Seán had told him he was heading off for a few days to the west of Ireland. He made no secret of his plans and, as the family later discovered, Seán consistently told those he met the truth about what he was doing and where he was going. The friend he met said he didn't seem stressed or in trouble. It was just a holiday.

To get to the west of Ireland by bus, you have to take a fairly circuitous route through Armagh and Cavan before going on to Galway. Seán's journey can be traced along this route where he took connecting buses.

The next day there was another coincidence. Seán reached Galway City and was walking through Eyre Square when, by complete chance, he bumped into his cousins from Donegal. It would have been fairly unusual for all of them to be in the city on the one day.

Again, the cousins weren't a bit alarmed by Seán's demeanour and they chatted amicably. He told them he was heading around Ireland 'to get his head cleared', and, of course, there was no suggestion at this stage that Seán was missing from home. He was quite open with them, the only bit he didn't mention was that he hadn't told his parents what he was doing or that they thought he had gone to school the previous day when he was actually setting off on his travels. The cousins assumed his parents knew exactly what he was doing.

It was a couple of days later before his cousins returned home to Donegal. They mentioned in passing that they had bumped into Seán in Eyre Square. Their mother knew at this stage that he was missing and she immediately contacted Seán's parents and told them of the chance encounter. Even then, there didn't seem to be any cause for alarm. Seán was well, he was in Galway and he had made no attempt to avoid his cousins nor had he tried to conceal what he was doing.

This gave some hope to his parents. Gerry went down to Galway and had a look around the city but didn't find any trace of Seán. On the Sunday, he went live on the local radio station, Galway Bay FM, to appeal to Seán to make contact with home. There was no word from Seán but a garda in Ennistymon in Co. Clare was listening in and he phoned the station.

The garda had a strange story to tell. He said he had been talking to Seán the previous night, Saturday, just five days into his journey.

Gerry travelled to Clare and met the garda who told him that a local fisherman from Doolin had been driving over the Cliffs of Moher at eleven o'clock on the Saturday night when he saw a lad out walking on his own. Because of the lateness of the hour, he turned his car and stopped and offered him a lift. Again, Seán made no attempt to conceal his identity or what he was about. He told the fisherman he had travelled from Co. Down and needed somewhere to stay the night so the fisherman dropped him into the village of Liscannor. He pointed out the local hostel where Seán could get a bed for the night.

It was the tail end of the holiday season, however, and there were still plenty of visitors about and beds may not have been very plentiful, particularly so late at night. In many hostels at that time of year, people arrive early in the day to reserve their sleeping accommodation so by that time of night it would have been very difficult to find some place to stay. It is not unknown in the fine weather for young people to sleep out in the countryside for the odd night and Seán had already left it very late to look for some place to stay.

The fisherman dropped Seán off near the hostel but he wasn't happy about leaving him. He sensed the lad was a bit depressed or something was wrong and he didn't want to leave until he had done something for him. So, as he was driving through Ennistymon, he stopped and told a garda the story about picking him up and said he was worried about him.

Later that night the patrol car spotted Seán, not in the village but in open countryside. The gardaí stopped and spoke to him and he told them there was no accommodation to be had in Liscannor. He had walked out of the town seeking a guesthouse. But, he said, there were dogs barking at him so he had decided to sleep out and then resume his journey to Cork the next day. The gardaí said he seemed fine, he was clean and well kept and again Seán made no attempt to conceal his identity, giving the gardaí his name and address.

But this is where the trail went cold. Seán had told the gardaí he was travelling on to Cork so that's where Gerry went. He firmly believed he was just one step behind his son but he never succeeded in catching up with him.

Arriving in Cork, Gerry again went on local radio to appeal to Seán to make contact with him. This time he took the search a bit further, putting up posters around the city. There was no response from his son to the radio broadcast and so Gerry went home to Downpatrick, physically tired and emotionally exhausted.

It is worth noting here that local radio stations around Ireland have been most generous in providing airtime to the families of the disappeared. They have been on chat shows and phone-ins and on news bulletins. Many of the searches have been publicised through local radio, bringing hundreds of people together to comb the countryside when people disappear. The great advantage of local radio is that people in a fairly specific area hear the news almost immediately and can react by joining a search party or searching their own lands. Also local radio has more time to give to families so a missing person story may get several bites of the airtime 'cherry'.

Over the following weeks and months, Gerry wrote to every newspaper in Ireland. He set up radio interviews and the story was broadcast on *Crimeline* on RTÉ. He also kept in touch with Doolin, travelling up and down and talking to people there because that was where the last definite sighting of Seán had been.

There are several strange things about Seán's disappearance. Although he never mentioned he was leaving, he made no secret of his journey when he bumped into an acquaintance in Belfast or his cousins in Galway or the fisherman in Doolin or the gardaí the same night. And it seems he had done his homework in relation to his itinerary, even checking out that there is a bus from Doolin to Cork.

Seán is described as a very quiet, very nice lad. He has a soft Northern accent and plenty of mates. He had been thinking of a career in social work.

Since his disappearance, his family doesn't know what to think. Gerry says they don't talk about it now 'but some days I think he's out there working in Cork'.

Then there are the sightings, some of which seemed so good at the time. There was a report from Tarbert in Co. Kerry that a Belfast lad had been asking about the ferry. He told a local shopkeeper he was getting the morning ferry. A garda car was there at the ferry the following morning but Seán didn't turn up.

Seán's brothers and sisters have all grown up since he left home, they're getting on with their lives and Seán doesn't know that he is now an uncle. 'There have been happy days', Gerry says, 'but you always wonder is there somebody who knows something, who knows what happened or where he is.'

His dad reasons that at some stage Seán must have been in a bar having a drink and a chat and he must have identified himself. 'He never denied who he was or what he was doing, even when he met the gardaí in Doolin.' Seán's parents see that as a very positive thing, the fact that Seán was so open about his movements.

Then there is always the possibility that something happened in Doolin and that Seán is dead. 'You can't say he's dead but he could be', his Dad agrees.

The family has faced the possibility that Seán could have fallen over the Cliffs of Moher during the night but Gerry has spoken to the local fishermen who told him that everything that goes over the cliffs comes back in again and, so far, there has been nothing.

The Doolin area is a prime tourist resort with many thousands of people visiting each year. It is a Mecca for music lovers and a place where young people from all over the world meet up. Could Seán have met up with somebody who offered him a lift to Cork or beyond? Or could he have decided to keep travelling with someone who was, like himself, passing through?

The search goes on, his family keep his case constantly in the media hoping, not only that Seán is alive, but also that he will get in touch with them at some stage. They also want anyone who knows anything about his disappearance that night to pass on whatever information they have.

14

Dan Ryan

'His eyes were sparkling. It was so real and I felt I was getting a message from him.'

Born Kilrush, Co Clare 1974.
Missing from New York since 15 August, 1998.

On 15 August, 1998, the world stood aghast at yet another atrocity in Northern Ireland – the bombing of Omagh. It was a day the Ryan family would never forget, although they had no connection with those killed and injured in the attack. They were thousands of miles away making a new life for themselves in New York. They had been there for 12 years but, on the day of the Omagh bombing, the Ryans were coming to terms with their own agony, the disappearance of their 24-year-old son, Dan.

Dan Ryan was born in England in 1974 but lived in Kilrush, Co. Clare until he was 12. Then, in 1986, the family emigrated to the United States where Dan lived in the family apartment in New York.

On the night of 15 August, 1998, Dan went to Billy and Bob's Sports Bar in the vicinity of 235th Street and White Plains Road in the Bronx. He was seen leaving the bar around 4 am and that was the last sighting of him. The barman remembered him, he said Dan was playing pool and that he was talking about joining a pool club in Yonkers.

Dan's mother, Agnes, remembers her son going out that night. 'I couldn't even talk about it for years', she says, 'he just went out to the pub and was playing pool. He wasn't the type to take off. He wouldn't have joined a cult or anything. He left the pub and nobody saw him after that.'

Although he worked in telemarketing by day, Dan's first love was music and he was an accomplished musician, playing the guitar and writing his own songs. While in school he won a number of talent contests and was a member of a band that also won prizes. Some of his work was recorded on tape and his sisters, his twin, Rachel, and his younger sister, Joanne, were proud of him.

All the signs were that Dan did not choose to disappear. The most telling sign was the fact that he left his beloved guitar behind along with his clothes and his passport. Leaving the passport behind was also important because it meant there was no way he had headed back to Ireland.

Four years later, in 2002, Dan's parents, Eugene and Agnes, returned to live in Ireland, although Joanne, who was in acting school in New York, stayed on. 'I couldn't stand it any more', says Agnes, 'I thought about it so much, I nearly went insane. Every thought that could go through my head did. Something happened him that night. I wonder will we ever hear the truth.'

When they realised Dan wasn't coming home, his parents started to search for him. They began by telephoning hospitals and morgues, hoping they would find their son, but also praying that he would be okay, that he would be alive. Agnes recalls that time as 'horrible'.

After Dan's disappearance, Agnes found it impossible to sleep. Then, three years ago, a strange thing happened. Agnes fell asleep on the sofa and dreamt that Dan was standing beside her. 'His eyes were sparkling', she recalls, 'it was so real and I felt I was getting a message from him'. 'Dan was smiling', she says, 'I always remember his eyes, big sparkly green eyes' and she says she got 'a little bit of peace' from the dream. After that the family decided to return to Ireland.

In the search for an answer as to why Dan disappeared, his sister, Joanne, joined the audience of the Sylvia Brown show on US TV. Joanne was given a reading by the psychic who told her that Dan had 'passed over'. The show upset Agnes who was watching at home. 'I was so mad', she says, 'it was the same old stuff, this woman was big into bi-polar disorder, just labelling people'. Agnes also admits that she found the search for Dan in the States 'dreadful'. 'They didn't give a damn. They weren't one bit helpful.'

Even though they have returned to Ireland, the search continues. The family watch anxiously when any likely leads emerge from the United States or when an unidentified body is found. That's the worst bit – the not knowing.

Today Eugene and Agnes live in Co. Clare. Their hope is that someday someone will make contact and throw some light on the mystery of what became of their beloved son.

15

Fiona Sinnott

'Something awful happened to her.'

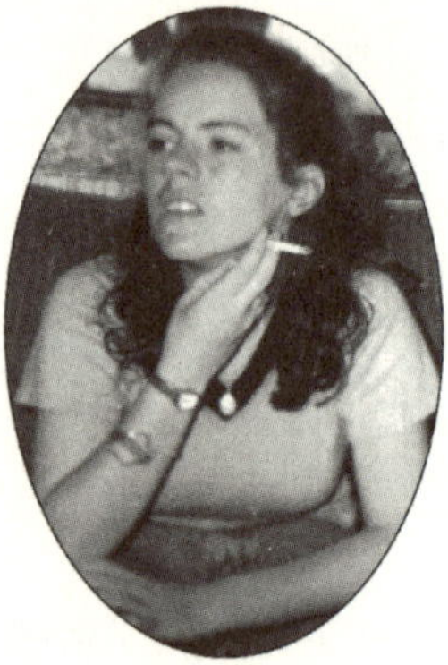

Born 1979.
Missing from Bridgetown, Co. Wexford since 9 February, 1998.

'Something awful happened to her'. Those are the words of Fiona Sinnott's sister, Diane, who is convinced that she is dead, that she died on the day she disappeared in February 1998.

Fiona was one of five children of Pat and Mary Sinnott. There were three girls, Diane, Caroline and Fiona and two boys, Séamus and Norman. The 19-year-old was the mother of a baby girl, Emma, but it hadn't always been easy for Fiona. Her family are quite upfront in describing how she had suffered a series of assaults from a boyfriend and had been taken to hospital several times. On each occasion, however, she discharged herself and got on with her life. She never pressed charges against anyone or disclosed who had been responsible.

there is a link with Fiona' says Diane, 'but she's not alive now. It's been too long. My parents think the same thing.'

The family travelled to the unveiling of the monument to the missing in Kilkenny. They are very conscious that Fiona is only one of many people who have gone without trace, seemingly vanished off the face of the earth and they empathise with the other families. They remember watching a television news report on the disappearance of Jo Jo Dullard, never thinking something like that could happen to their own family.

Today the Sinnotts see little of Emma. She is being raised by her father's parents, Kitty and Seán Carroll.

The bottom line now is that the family have appealed again and again for someone to speak up, to tell somebody what they know about Fiona, 'they don't even have to give their names, we just want to find her body', says Diane.

16

Ciara Breen

'Other families forgive. I will never forgive.'

Born 1979.
Missing from Dundalk since 13 February, 1997.

Ciara Breen was just 17 when she disappeared. She went missing from the family home in Dundalk on the 13 February, 1997. Ciara's mother, Bernadette, will never forget that fateful night six years ago when Ciara sneaked out without her knowledge to meet up with friends.

Bernadette discovered that Ciara had slipped out when she woke up in the middle of the night. She popped into Ciara's bedroom to find her gone and the window wide open. Her immediate thought as she looked at the open window and the empty bed was: 'This one's caught now.' Ciara had friends that her mother did not like her hanging around with and Bernadette guessed that the teenager had slipped out to meet up with these friends, without saying anything to her mother. Bernadette discovered that her daughter was not in her room shortly before 2 am.

Bernadette decided to go downstairs and wait for Ciara. She didn't know how long Ciara had been gone, as she hadn't heard her leave. She waited for her daughter to return, counting the minutes passing, not imagining for a moment that Ciara was never going to come back. After two long hours waiting for her daughter to return, Bernadette moved upstairs to continue her wait. She was anxious not to panic; she expected Ciara to come in at any minute and she wanted to give her daughter the chance to come home before taking dramatic action and calling in the police. But as the hours passed and Ciara did not show up, Bernadette began to think that there was something not quite right. When early morning set in and there was still no sign of her, Bernadette got very worried and couldn't hold off any longer. Ciara would not have stayed out all night, especially if she didn't want her mum to know she was meeting up with friends that she didn't want her to socialise with. Bernadette tried to cancel an appointment she had that day and called the police in to launch a search.

The Gardaí came out immediately when they received Bernadette's call. 'The Dundalk Gardaí were great, they couldn't have done more', recalls Bernadette. Although she hadn't been aware of it, following the police investigation it was discovered that this was not the first time Ciara had slipped out – it turned out she had slipped out a couple of times before. Bernadette did not particularly approve of the girls Ciara was hanging out with, hence it seemed the teenager thought it better to keep it a secret from her mother when she was meeting up with them. Despite the fact that Bernadette did not want her daughter seeing the girls in question, she is extremely grateful for all of the help they gave after Ciara went missing: 'Even though I didn't approve, they were very helpful and I'm very grateful to them for that.'

A search was launched that morning, 14 February. One of the first things they did was put posters of Ciara up everywhere. Bernadette thought of all the kinds of places her daughter frequented, like discos, and posters were put up in these locations. She hoped that someone who knew Ciara would see the poster and remember seeing her on the night of 13 February and maybe give the police some clue that may lead to finding her.

They launched radio appeals on the local radio station, convinced that there had to be someone out there who knew something, someone who would come forward on hearing the appeal. All of their search efforts appeared to be futile, however, and nothing came out of it. There were many reported sightings but upon investigation they revealed no further clues to what had happened to Ciara. There was even a videotape sent over from England by a person who was convinced that they recognised Ciara in it. But once again, Bernadette's heart sank when she viewed the tape with the Dundalk Gardaí and they realised that it wasn't the missing Ciara. They had met with a dead end once again.

To make matters even worse, Bernadette had an appointment the day that Ciara went missing, during which she received horrific news: 'My daughter went missing and I found out I had cancer on the same day.'

Bernadette had more than enough bad news to cope with and Ciara was not even around to turn to for comfort. Bernadette's closest ally had disappeared without trace. Although Bernadette didn't know it immediately, the guards came to the conclusion that Ciara was dead quite early on.

A man who was older than Ciara was arrested, but the DPP decided there was no evidence to prosecute him and he was released. Although it's very difficult for Bernadette to come to terms with it, she now believes that Ciara was murdered the night she disappeared.

Bernadette is devastated and angry about what she believes to have been the fate of her beautiful young daughter. She thinks the worst happened: 'I think she went out and died horribly. I think she was murdered. That's what the guards think as well. They are convinced of it.' The belief is that Ciara's body is somewhere in the area but when a search was conducted for a body, nothing was found.

Bernadette has no doubt that someone out there must know something about what happened to Ciara and she is furious that, despite all the appeals and the desperate suffering that her disappearance has caused, no one has come forward with information that might lead to finding her. What she cannot understand is that somebody could be getting up every morning, knowing the truth, knowing that they could end the nightmare of being stuck in limbo, but instead choosing to protect the perpetrator by keeping their silence. 'Someone out there definitely knows something, but all the begging in the world isn't going to do anything. They won't come forward. If Ciara was murdered by some guy, he will do it again and, if he does, I hope his protector feels okay about it.'

Bernadette knows that she could never forgive whoever was responsible for Ciara's murder, assuming that is what happened. That person or those persons took Bernadette's most precious possession from her, her only child. 'Other families forgive. I'll never forgive whoever did this and I hope he rots in hell.'

Ciara has been missing for over six years now and her mother says that, although she felt Ciara was dead pretty early on, she was unable to admit it to herself until the last two to three years. It was too difficult to accept that something so horrible could have happened to the child she had brought into the world and raised for 17 years. Without Ciara, Bernadette is consumed by a great emptiness. She was so close to her daughter, who was also a great friend and she misses her desperately. The immense happiness she had when Ciara was around disappeared the night she went missing and there is nothing that could ever bring it back.

'It was just me and my daughter at home. I am devastated without Ciara. No matter how many people are around you, it's still desperately lonely. We were very good friends. I was a very, very happy woman. I loved my daughter so much.'

Every memory Bernadette has of Ciara is special. She remembers her continually happy disposition, her friendly nature, and, above all, the sound of her laughter. Ciara was always in good form, always on the lookout for humour, 'She was a messer, her thoughts would be "how can I get Mum this week?"' Bernadette remembers her daughter's extremely generous spirit. Ciara was also a kind person, always ready to help. Her mother recalls a time when they were standing waiting for a bus and saw a stray dog across the road. Ciara couldn't bear to see the hungry dog without doing anything and she crossed the road to go into the butchers where she bought a quarter pound of mince with her own pocket money and fed it to the dog. Ciara had a soft heart when it came to animals. She loved all types of animal and had lots of pets. The house was always full of animals – cats, dogs and rabbits.

Ciara was a devoted music fan. She loved listening to all kinds of music and always had some piece playing. Her taste was vast, ranging from classical to dance. Particularly poignant in the wake of her disappearance was the discovery of the last two pieces of music that Ciara ever listened to. One of these was a piece by Rachmaninov, which was found in her CD player while Toni Braxton's 'Unbreak my Heart' was in her tape player. They remain there to this very day.

At 17 years of age, Ciara was the youngest of the girls to disappear in Ireland. She had her whole life ahead of her and at the time of her disappearance she had been deciding which career path to follow. She had been studying computers but was very keen on doing a beauty course. She had great ideas when it came to beauty and Bernadette would have been delighted to support her in whatever she chose to do.

Ciara's maternal grandparents were also hit hard by the news of her disappearance. They were very close to Ciara as she and Bernadette had lived with them during her childhood years: 'We all loved Ciara so much. We lived with my parents until she turned 12.' She was very close to her grandfather, Brendan Coburn, who died three and a half years ago. Bernadette turned to her parents for comfort over the difficult years since Ciara disappeared and, in particular, her father provided huge strength and support. 'He was my rock and my friend through all this' says Bernadette.

Over the years of searching for Ciara and dealing with her loss, Bernadette has come to realise that there is very little done for families in situations like hers. She has hit out at a number of government authorities for their apparent lack of care for the families of missing people. She feels they have done little or nothing to ease their plight. 'As time goes on, I get angrier and angrier. Our kids are out there somewhere and as far as I can see our government doesn't give a damn. I'm very angry.'

Bernadette is anxious, however, to commend the Dundalk Gardaí. 'The Gardaí in Dundalk have been great. I have had absolutely no problems with them. They have gone above and beyond with their help, they were great.'

Bernadette is no longer expecting Ciara to turn up alive. She has come to terms with what she sees as the dreaded reality. Like the Dundalk Gardaí, Bernadette expects to find a body, and she feels it will be in the local area, not too far away from where Ciara went missing. Bernadette is now anxious to find her daughter's body and do the last thing she will ever be able to do for Ciara: 'I want to give her a proper burial. It's the last thing I can do for her.'

It is very difficult for Bernadette to talk about Ciara. She says she can, but prefers just to sit alone and think about her, 'Her life has been made so public'. Every memory she has of her 17-year-old daughter is a good one: 'My memories of Ciara are very happy and proud. She made me one of the happiest women alive over 17 years.'

Perhaps the most special memory that Bernadette will always treasure is the last words her daughter ever spoke to her 'The night she went missing, I had said I hoped I'd wake up in the morning for work. Ciara's reply, the last words she ever spoke to me were: "Don't worry Mum I will wake you up – I love you." I have that.'

Ciara and her mum had a policy never to go to bed angry. Naturally, they had their hassles, Ciara was a teenager, Bernadette was a mum, but they stuck rigidly to their agreement to always make up before going to bed.

Bernadette's suffering will never end. Day by day she wakes up tortured by the fact that Ciara is not there. Perhaps, even more painful, is the endless bewilderment of not knowing where Ciara is. If she even had a body, it would provide closure. Until the day that Bernadette finally discovers what happened, until she can finally lay her daughter to rest, she will be in an agonising limbo.

Bernadette sees it as utterly unjust that her daughter's life was cut short, so suddenly. She was so young, so beautiful and had so much going for her.

'Ciara was a beautiful girl who deserved to live life to the full and never got the opportunity', her mum says.

17

Fiona Pender

'Missing – Fiona and Baby. Remember me in your Prayers.'

Born July 1971.
Missing from Tullamore, Co. Offaly since 22 August, 1996.

In a house in Connolly Park in Tullamore, there is a bag packed ready for the maternity hospital, ready for a young woman who is almost eight months pregnant and waiting to give birth to her first child.

The tan coloured bag has been packed for seven years now. But it's not going anywhere. The little babygros and matinee jackets it contains belong to a baby long dead, a baby who died with its mother. The puzzle is – where is their grave? Have they been buried in rough countryside? Do mother and child lie at the bottom of a lake or river? Will they ever have a Christian burial?

This is the story of 25-year-old Fiona Pender, who disappeared on 22 August, 1996, when she was almost eight months pregnant.

Fiona's mother, Josephine, describes how the two of them were shopping on that Thursday evening in the Bridge Centre in Tullamore. 'We bought some more clothes for the baby. Fiona realised she would probably be living out of town once she had the baby so she was getting in all her little bits, like gripe water and Milton and all that crack. We left her at seven o'clock on the Thursday evening, I kissed her and that's the last time I saw her. I still remember her little face at the door. Fiona was in good form, looking forward to the birth of the baby, we were all looking forward to it, it was new life after Mark, my son, died 14 months earlier.'

In 1995, Josephine and her husband Seán had three children, Fiona, the eldest at 24 and the only girl, Mark, who was two years younger and John, who was 10 years younger. But Josephine, who always wanted a big family, says she should have had seven children. She suffered two miscarriages after Fiona and another two after Mark. When she eventually became pregnant with John, she was in danger of losing him too and had to spend three months in hospital. But all went well and she says jokingly that John was worth it.

In June 1995, Mark was 22 and engaged to be married to Gillian, the mother of his three-year-old son, Dean. They were planning their wedding for the following May in Durrow Church.

Mark and Fiona both loved motorbikes and, one sunny day, Mark and one his friends went for a spin in the countryside outside Tullamore. They stopped for an ice cream at a petrol station at Killeigh. When they set off again, the bearing went on the back wheel of Mark's bike and it went out of control, crashing into a lorry. The passenger was just slightly injured but Mark was killed.

Fiona was very close to her younger brother. He had introduced her to her boyfriend, John Thompson, who was also interested in bikes.

After Mark's death, Fiona decided to take part in one more bike rally in memory of her brother. She got a bad fright when she skidded and came off her bike outside the graveyard where Mark was buried and decided then to get rid of the bike.

But what to do with Mark's own bike? The Penders decided to bury the bike along with Mark's biking gear at a secret location in the Slieve Bloom Mountains. The entire family loved the mountains and decided this would be a fitting tribute. So they headed off for Clonaslee and buried the motorbike somewhere in the area. Only the family know the exact location of the burial, in a spot they used to love.

However, they have a strong feeling now that Fiona and her baby could be buried somewhere in the remote valleys and gorges and as a result, Josephine says they have 'a terrible feeling' about the mountains they used to enjoy.

After the horror of Mark's death, Fiona's baby was going to bring some new life into the family. 'This is a baby house', says Josephine, 'We love babies in this house. A cross baby would always stay quiet for my husband. They really took to him and I've always minded children.'

'I was due to come down town on Friday morning and I said to Fiona on the Thursday, I won't bother you, have a sleep on and I'll contact you later on. She said no, if you're down Mammy, just call. So I just gave a quick call and there was no answer. Now she had friends over from the States at the time on holidays, and I thought she was out with them. I went back down in the afternoon and she still wasn't there, but I didn't panic, she still could have been out with the girls for the day or whatever.'

By Sunday there was still no sign of her so Josephine rang Fiona's boyfriend, John Thompson, who said he thought Fiona was at her parent's home. Together with John, Josephine went to Fiona's flat. There was no sign of anything amiss, no break in, no sign of a struggle and the things they had bought for the baby were still there.

Then they went to the graveyard in Durrow, hoping that Fiona had gone to visit Mark's grave, but there was no sign of her. Fiona had often visited her brother's grave, sometimes even late at night.

They then checked the hospital in case Fiona had needed medical attention or had gone into early labour, but she wasn't there and, they reasoned, it would have been very strange if she had been admitted and the hospital hadn't tried to contact any of them. Fiona had had problems during the early months of her pregnancy but was well out of the woods at this stage, and she had been assured the baby was healthy and well.

Next, Josephine and Seán and their son John, together with John Thompson, went to the Gardaí and reported Fiona missing. 'The gardaí pointed out that she was 25 and was an adult. It wasn't really taken seriously I suppose until the Monday', says Josephine. 'Then the searching really started with sub aqua divers and dogs and they found absolutely nothing.'

The Gardaí searched the Bord na Mona silt ponds, the local lakes, river, canal, woodlands and open countryside. They even checked that she hadn't been buried in her brother's grave.

The Penders themselves decided to search the area in the Slieve Bloom Mountains where they had buried Mark's motorcycle gear after his death. They thought that maybe Fiona had gone there, but there was no trace of her.

There had been no indication that Fiona had planned to go away, her bank account and her credit union account weren't touched.

Josephine, desperate now, brought in diviners, earth energy practitioners and psychics from the UK, but they couldn't find anything either.

The last sighting of Fiona was at 6 am on Friday, 23 August when her boyfriend, John Thompson, said goodbye to her before leaving for work on his family's farm about eight miles away.

It is hard to imagine that further tragedy could strike the Penders, but it did. Josephine takes up the story.

'My husband, ah, he found it very hard, he just went down so low he couldn't come back. He cried for his children every night you know and prayed and prayed. He just went deeper and deeper and didn't come out of it. John and myself came home from work one evening at five o'clock and he was after hanging himself.

'My son found my husband upstairs. We thought he was in the garden. He was trying to dig the garden, he loved his garden, he always had it dug, drilled and the potatoes and the onions and whatever sowed by 17th March. So it was late for him to do it and he was gone so weak he looked like a man who had cancer or a very long illness or something.

'John screamed and said "Mammy, Mammy, don't come up, Daddy's after hanging himself". Of course the first thing I did was race up and John said "get me a knife, get me a knife". So I went down and got a knife and John got up into the attic and cut him down. He was absolutely marvellous.

'My husband was still warm when I held him. I never ever blamed Seán for what he did because it was the next thing he had to do, it was the only thing he could do. To me, he was just sick and he died of a broken heart.

'We brought him back home from the morgue and we waked him here and he looked 20 years younger. I was never angry with him for doing it because I understood why he did it. But you couldn't be angry with him when you seen him looking so happy and so content.

'The only sadness I have is that I wasn't with him, that he felt that bad and that he was on his own. And that's the same with Fiona and with Mark, I wasn't with any of them when they died.'

The family sitting-room walls are covered in Seán's paintings. 'Seán was a fabulous artist, he generally did landscapes, he loved to do snow scenes. He attempted to paint the Mona Lisa years ago and he left it and then about four years before he died, he attempted it again and it turned out absolutely marvellous. People come in and say it's better than the original! It's really lovely to have them now and at the Offertory at his funeral I brought up one of his paintings.'

Also in that sitting room are the family photographs. Seán, Mark and Fiona all smile out from happier times. There are glossy photos of Fiona, who worked part-time as a model. She also worked as a hairdresser. After she got rid of her motorbike, she bought a little Mini and travelled to people's homes to do their hair.

In her heart Josephine believes that Fiona is dead, 'Fiona and myself were extremely close. I spent five and six hours at a time in the Garda barracks at the start going over things and giving statements. They were saying that having me there was nearly as good as having Fiona in the barracks, because we were so close. People might think well, she didn't tell you everything, but she did', she says with a little conspiratorial laugh.

The mystery of what happened to Fiona is still unsolved. Where did she go? Did she leave her flat and meet someone? Was she abducted? There was no sign of a violent struggle in the flat. Did that mean she knew her abductor? That thought makes it even worse for her family, that somebody she trusted would abduct and probably murder her.

It is also very hard for her family and friends to understand that anyone could murder a pregnant woman, killing not only Fiona but her unborn child as well. And given that it might have been someone who knew her, then they would have known of the tragedy of Mark's death and how the Penders were looking forward so much to this new life. Tullamore is not a big place and most people would have known of Mark's death.

'If Fiona were alive, she wouldn't let me worry', says Josephine. 'If she was going to a party or wouldn't be home on time, she would always ring, she would never let me worry, especially since Mark died.'

The only other scenario her mother can imagine is 'if someone had her and she wasn't able to contact me, but it's seven years now. Fiona couldn't be alive and not contact me. I believe and I feel in myself that Fiona is dead.'

Fiona's baby was due on 22 October and around that date Gardaí checked with all the maternity hospitals in this country and in England to see if anyone matching her description had given birth to a baby. Again they came up with nothing.

All Josephine wants now is to find her daughter's body and that of her unborn baby. 'More than having them [whoever killed Fiona] punished, I don't care about that really because we all have a day of reckoning and we'll all answer for what we did or didn't do, so what I really want is to find Fiona and her baby and to lay them to rest. I don't want her lying out there somewhere, she was too good and too precious. I want to find Fiona in my lifetime, so that John won't have to have to deal with it on his own.'

Josephine plans to bury her daughter with her dad and her brother in the grave in Durrow. 'I know if it was me, she'd go to the ends of the earth to find me, and I'll never stop either', says Josephine.

And she has this message for anyone withholding information about what happened to Fiona or where her body is buried. 'You have a Christian duty if you know anything to come forward and to say what you know, even at this stage. People can't disappear off the face of the earth and no one knowing what happened to them. And I know myself that people do know and they don't just care enough to come forward.'

Josephine has kept all of Fiona's things, all her clothes and all her private little bits and pieces. 'I won't think of getting rid of those until I find her' she says, 'I feel I would be betraying her if I did'.

'I have her case that she packed ready for the hospital, with all the baby's things in it and all the matinee coats I knitted for her in it. She had a nappy bag for the baby and she had all her little bits for the baby in that and that's there and I'll never get rid of it.'

In August of 2003, Fiona had been missing for seven years, which meant that she could be officially declared dead. Josephine didn't want that, she wants to find Fiona first. But on 22 August, Josephine and John went to the grave in Durrow with a little plaque bearing the inscription: 'Missing – Fiona and Baby. Remember me in your Prayers'.

The Pender family has now been reduced to two, Josephine and her remaining son John. They are close friends and John has grown into a kind and dependable young man who has had to deal with the worst horrors of the adult world at too young an age. He was just 12 when Mark was killed, 14 when Fiona disappeared and just a couple of weeks off his 17th birthday on the day that he cut his own father down from the attic where he had hanged himself.

Today John is 20 and at college, studying art and design. He has inherited his father's artistic talents and is a promising artist.

18

Denis Walsh

'Denis was very frightened of the hospital.'

Born 4 September, 1972.
Missing from Limerick City since 9 March, 1996.

His association with the city of Limerick and its mental hospital may well have been the trigger that caused 24-year-old Denis Walsh to disappear on 9 March, 1996. There was no suggestion he was leaving, he just got up and left one day with about fifty pounds in his pocket, his passport untouched.

At the time of his disappearance, Denis Walsh was studying accountancy and doing very well academically, but he found it difficult to cope with the pressure of third-level study. He suffered from depression and had been hospitalised a number of times.

Denis had not been a cause of concern to his parents until the age of 18 when, they say, he suffered some kind of a breakdown. They got professional advice and Denis was admitted to hospital. However, he hated the hospital and his parents are very critical of what they perceive to be the way he was treated.

'It is an ordeal for parents, it is the most heartbreaking thing to have to admit your son or daughter to a mental hospital', Denis's mother, Mary, says. And today she feels that the memory of being hospitalised could be what is keeping him away, 'that's what Limerick means to Denis'.

'Denis was very frightened of the hospital', recalls Mary, 'the last time he was there, they kept him in for three weeks. I felt that they filled him with drugs and gave him very little counselling. He was in a room with much older people.'

When his parents visited Denis in hospital, they found it very difficult, 'you just couldn't talk to him, he was filled with drugs, he was completely out of it. We sent Denis into hospital to get treatment and thinking our son would come home, not perfect, but that in time he would be well. But there was nothing done for him, there was no progress made in the three weeks that he was there.'

Mary is also very critical of the lack of follow-up treatment when Denis was discharged from hospital. 'It was a big step to come home, to go out into the environment away from the hospital and I would have expected some follow up, someone calling to see how he was doing, but there was nothing.'

She was also surprised to see that Denis was sent home with numerous pills to take. 'When a person is depressed, it is so difficult to know how they are and you rely on the experts. Denis was sent home with this load of drugs and you had to make sure he took them but Denis rebelled against taking the tablets.'

Mary says her youngest son was 'kind and gentle'. There was no question of his illness making him aggressive or violent. 'We never had cause to fear him at all, he just got very hyper, very anxious.'

The Walsh family hoped that after the first breakdown when he was 18 that Denis would pick up 'but that didn't happen, he just went downhill and he ended up in hospital on several occasions'. They are also very critical of the hospital where Denis was treated. 'There is a modern psychiatric hospital in the Regional in Limerick but there is also St. Joseph's and it hasn't moved on in the last fifty years. It was disgraceful to put any young person in there. It broke our hearts to see him in there', says Mary, 'I wouldn't wish it on anybody.' When they asked why he couldn't be treated in the modern psychiatric wing in the Regional, Mary was told that there were too many doors and he might be able to get out.

Denis had only been home for a couple of days when he went missing. He hadn't been fully discharged and was due to go back to the hospital on the Monday for a check-up before he would be officially discharged. He had a dread of going back, and he had told people many times that this would be his last time in there.

On the Saturday he went missing, Denis had breakfast with his mother. 'He was a bit agitated', she says, 'he wasn't that well.'

Mary stresses that she and her family really felt they were doing the best thing for Denis by sending him into hospital. Even the experts told them not to try and handle something that they didn't understand by themselves.

Around 11 o'clock Denis left the house to go into town. It was a normal goodbye as he left to get the bus. Mary told him she'd see him in the evening and would have his favourite dinner of boiled bacon ready for him. Denis smiled and headed off. Mary had no inkling that anything was wrong that morning. Denis was tidy and clean and she wasn't concerned.

Today the family agonise over who Denis met on that fateful trip into Limerick. 'He definitely spoke to someone', says Mary, 'I have appealed to anyone who knows anything to tell us what he had planned or who he went away with.' Even the local TD, Willie O'Dea, went on local radio to ask anyone with information to come forward, anonymously if they preferred.

Denis was very religious in a searching kind of way. 'He was into Buddhism when he went missing, Denis was searching for answers.' For this reason his parents wonder if Denis met up with members of a religious cult or even new age travellers and just went away with them. At that time, such a move might have seemed a very attractive option when weighed against going back into the psychiatric hospital he hated. His parents are completely convinced that Denis had no plans to take his own life.

In the first six months after he disappeared, there were several reported sightings of Denis, some around Limerick and also in Ennis and Dublin. Denis was still in Limerick city for at least three days after he left home. The manageress of a coffee shop called the family to say that Denis had been there. She knew him to see and she also told the family that he had been reading a book on Buddhism in the coffee shop.

There was another sighting which is also believed to have been genuine. It was at the end of May in Belfast at the Seacat terminal. A security guard there recognised Denis from seeing his picture on RTÉ's *Crimeline*. Denis bought a ticket for the following day's sailing and the guard noticed him because he looked like he had been sleeping rough. The family now says that they are very disappointed that they left the follow up to the Gardaí and wish they had taken some sort of action themselves, because the young man, whoever he was, cancelled the ticket and didn't sail.

There was another possible sighting in Cork at the 1996 Tall Ships Festival when Denis was seen in the company of a new age traveller. The family travelled to Cork and searched for Denis but to no avail. 'It doesn't go away, but we're stronger now. We grieved something terrible.'

Denis is the youngest of five children of Mary and Denis Walsh. He has three brothers, Paul, Jim and Michael and a sister, Anne. There have been many family events since 1996 and Denis has been sorely missed. All of his siblings have married and there are three new grandchildren. When his only sister, Anne, married five years ago she appealed for Denis to return home.

The family has also gone to see various psychics for advice. The first one had bad news and told them that Denis was dead. 'It was so awful we didn't want to think about it.' The family then travelled to Dublin to see another psychic and this time were given good news, that their son was still alive. The first one upset them and the second one cancelled that out, so they decided not to heed either one of them.

With no positive leads, it's very hard to keep going from day to day. 'It just hits you. Sometimes I would see somebody resembling Denis but it's not him. You get up with it in the morning and go to bed with it at night', says Mary.

Denis' parents say they still have faith that he will return home someday. 'We've left Denis in the hands of God at this stage and hope he will make contact with us. One day I think he's alive… it is awful trying to cope but we never let the rest of the family down. We are a very close family', says Mary.

There is, of course, a gnawing need in Mary to know what happened to her son. 'I keep asking myself if he is alive, is he happy? Is he suffering from loss of memory? Does he even remember our phone number?'

19

Jo Jo Dullard

'You don't think this can happen to your family.'

Born 1974.
Missing from Moone en route to Callan since 9 November, 1995.

The disappearance of Jo Jo Dullard on 9 November, 1995, has become one of the most high-profile missing person cases in Ireland, constantly in the news even after so many years. Much of this is due to Mary Phelan's work in keeping her sister Jo Jo's name constantly in the media and also to the setting up of the Garda initiative, Operation Trace, in 1998. This operation was aimed at investigating the disappearances of six women who went missing in the Leinster area over a five-year period. It is still not known whether any of the cases are linked, although the investigation continues and any new information which might connect the women is constantly being monitored.

What makes the disappearances of these six women different from other cases is that each of them vanished very suddenly, shortly after they had spoken with a family member or a friend or were sighted just a short distance from their homes. They took nothing with them, didn't touch their bank or post office accounts and had given no cause for concern before they disappeared. Each of them had friends, a loving family and seemed to be content with their lives. Some of them were on the verge of change, for example, Fiona Pender was soon to give birth to her first child and Jo Jo Dullard was returning home to begin a new job.

Jo Jo Dullard was 21 years old at the time of her disappearance. She had just moved home from Dublin to live in Callan in Co. Kilkenny but had spent that day in Dublin collecting her last dole payment. She then did some shopping and met friends before setting out to return to Callan. She had found a new job as a waitress in a restaurant in the town and, ironically, it was when she didn't turn up for work that the alarm was raised.

Jo Jo missed the last bus to Callan so took the bus to Naas, which was still more than fifty miles from Callan. She then started to hitch a lift in the direction of Kilkenny. This wasn't so unusual, it was something she had done before. It has to be remembered that in many rural areas hitching is still a way of life and, despite the warnings, many people continue to hitch lifts home by day and sometimes even at night as well. Of course, as may have been the case in Jo Jo's situation, some people hitch lifts but only get into a car when they know the driver.

That night Jo Jo first got a short lift as far as Kilcullen, followed by another to Moone in Co. Kildare. This would bring her in the direction of Carlow, but that was okay because it would bring her close to a friend's house where she could stay the night if necessary and continue on home the following morning.

When she arrived in Moone, Jo Jo phoned her friend, Mary Cullinane, and told her that she had missed the bus. They were chatting when Jo Jo asked Mary to hold on for a moment and then came back to the phone box and confirmed that she had a lift. Today there is a memorial stone beside the phone box to mark that last fateful call.

That was the last time anyone spoke to or heard from Jo Jo.

There was a sighting a short time later of a woman answering her description leaning in the back door of a dark-coloured Toyota Carina type car, but the driver or occupants of this car have never been traced.

But where did she go from Moone? There were reported sightings of a woman who could have been Jo Jo in the village of Castledermot just before midnight.

When Jo Jo failed to reach home, or to turn up for work the next evening, her sister, Kathleen, raised the alarm.

They are a close-knit family of three sisters, Kathleen, Mary and Nora, and a brother, Tom. Jo Jo's father died before she was born and her mother just 10 years later. This meant that Jo Jo was raised by her older sister, Kathleen, and when Kathleen married, Jo Jo went to live with her and her new husband.

Jo Jo became very close to Kathleen's children, more of a sister than an aunt. When she was 16 she went to live with another sister, Mary Phelan, and became very close to Mary's children, Imelda, who was then eight years old, and Melvin, who was five at the time. Mary says they still miss her terribly and remember her well.

From the day Jo Jo disappeared, her family has done everything to keep her in the public eye. There have been articles, photographs, press conferences, posters and appeals. They have enlisted the help of politicians, the media and friends. They have searched everywhere that she could possibly be.

On the first Christmas Day after Jo Jo's disappearance, in 1995, they hadn't the heart to celebrate, although they made sure Santa came to the kids. They then went out and spent the day searching the fields and ditches and walking the roads around Moone. They remember it as a lonely day, a day when they felt excluded from the normal celebrations of Christmas and a day when they missed Jo Jo terribly.

It hit the members of her family then that despite the tragedy in their own personal lives, the world continued to revolve, people continued to go about their business and they felt very much on the periphery of it all.

It was Moone that hosted the first special Mass for missing people under the auspices of the newly-established Jo Jo Dullard Memorial Trust. Mary and her husband Martin set up the trust with the assistance of local TD, John McGuinness.

Jo Jo's family were also instrumental in the erection of a National Monument for Missing People in the grounds of Kilkenny Castle. The monument, which carries the handprints of members of the families of Ireland's missing people, was unveiled in May 2002. Many of the families were there.

President Mary McAleese attended the ceremony. Mary Phelan told those present that the unveiling of the monument was a major source of comfort to families who had experienced pain and suffering following the disappearance of a loved one. 'We have no grave', she said, 'so it is very important to us. It is a sad yet very happy day. The families of missing persons have nowhere to grieve – this monument really helps because it gives you a place to put flowers. This is not closure for me but it is a source of comfort.'

Mary went on to say that Ireland urgently needs to set up specialised Missing Persons Units throughout the country. 'We should have units in all the regions', she said, 'if you hear of a missing person in another country, the first word out of their family's mouths is "specialised units". People come to their door straight away and offer assistance. They also get counselling and support.'

The new monument consists of a tall column of cast bronze hands featuring the handprints of family members of missing persons. It is hoped that it will serve as a permanent reminder to the public of the people who have disappeared and that it will also form a focal point for the families.

Mary and Martin Phelan, along with John McGuinness, are now campaigning for the establishment of a specialist Missing Persons

Unit, which would be activated as soon as someone was reported missing. They have also travelled to the US, where they met the FBI and looked at search techniques used there (see Chapter 5).

Mary told me she is convinced that Jo Jo is dead, that she was murdered on the night she disappeared: 'I know she's dead, I knew from day one.' Mary says Jo Jo's disappearance should have been treated as a murder case from that day. 'There are cases in New York and Australia where they were able to bring in a suspect without having a body', she says.

Mary recalls a time when she felt that something so awful only happened to other people. 'When Annie McCarrick went missing, my heart went out to that poor family. Then it all died down and I thought she had been found. Then Jo Jo went missing and I saw her picture beside Annie's and I got such a shock. You don't think this can happen to your family.'

Mary is adamant that not enough is being done to find the people who have disappeared over the years, many of them young women. She believes that a specialist unit would be able to find evidence before it goes cold, to locate passers-by who might remember seeing something in the hours following a disappearance and in doing so prevent the escape of those who abduct and murder some of the most vulnerable.

All of this stems from the heartache, from the desperation of losing a loved one and of not knowing what happened to them. For Jo Jo, all Mary wants now is 'to be able to give her a Christian burial alongside her Mam and Dad'.

The National Monument for Missing People in the grounds of Kilkenny Castle, which shows the handprints of members of the families of Ireland's missing people

20

Michael Farrell

'Michael doesn't even know he is a grandfather.'

Born 10 December, 1963.
Missing since 19 September, 1994.

Sometimes people who go missing ring home, say nothing and just listen to hear a loved one's voice. That is the hope that Margaret Farrell has clung to since a mysterious call to her home in the early hours in 2001.

On 19 September, 1994, the ferry *Isle of Inishmore* was travelling from Rosslare on Ireland's south coast to Pembroke in Wales. Michael Farrell, a 30-year old from Donaghmede in Dublin, was the manager of the on-board cinema. He had been working and chatting to various crew members during the night, none of whom noticed anything unusual. Around 10.30 pm, at the end of the screening, he walked out of the ticket office of the cinema towards the crew accommodation. He met other crew members and they asked him how things were going. 'Very slow', he told them, which meant there weren't that many passengers on board. This was the last time Michael was seen on the ship.

At 11.15 pm he was due to show another film, but there was no sign of him. Passengers were waiting to view the film and so Michael's name was called over the public address system, but he didn't respond. When Michael couldn't be found, a search of the ship got underway immediately, but there was still no sign of him and, when the boat docked in Pembroke, the Master of Arms informed the Captain and they went and searched the ship again. The Welsh police and the coastguard were informed at 7.35 am.

Michael's dad, also called Michael, has great praise for the Welsh police. 'They sent us a copy of the report that they received and they even invited us over for a weekend to join them', he says.

'There was a sea search carried out by the Welsh police and the coastguard. They put out two helicopters and two lifeboats. I have copies of their reports here in front of me. They searched for two hours, they call it a "box" search. They went in as far as possible to the shore and they found nothing.'

Michael had worked with Irish Ferries for nine years and today his father cannot understand what happened. He is proud of his son's seaman's record and thumbs through reports. 'Ability very good, general conduct very good', it reads and then suddenly, there are just blank pages. 'That's it, just blank pages', says Michael, 'it's like the house here and his own house, just blank. But we remember him in every room of the house.'

So what happened to him? 'Honest truth, I haven't got a clue. He was in good form, he wasn't short of money, and he didn't drink much. I think he had had about two pints on the night he disappeared.'

Michael is married to Anita and has three children, a girl and two boys, now ranging from 22 down to 13 years. His daughter, Lisa, now has a baby of her own, Hannah, who was born on Christmas Eve

2002. It is a great source of sadness to his parents that Michael doesn't know how his own kids have progressed or even that he is a grandfather. And his children miss him enormously. 'I wish there was some way of getting word to him, of telling him about Lisa's baby, but we don't know if he went over the side of the ship or what happened that night.'

His parents' gut instinct is that their son is still alive. 'I just have to keep saying that to myself, that he is still alive, I have to hope, to live in hope.' They pin those hopes on a phone call they received in 2001. Michael's parents were asleep when the phone rang at ten minutes to three in the morning. Michael Senior takes up the story: 'The phone rang but when I answered, there was nobody there. It rang again, there were three calls in ten minutes. We have caller ID in the hall and I wrote down the number. It was a mobile phone with a Belfast number and when I rang it, a girl said "hello" and then cut me off. I rang her again and told her my son was missing and that I hoped the call had something to do with him, but she denied ringing our number.'

Michael Snr still believes that the call could have come from his son, that suddenly in the small hours of the night he felt a pang of homesickness or wondered how his elderly parents were and just wanted to hear their voices. Margaret says she has heard this can happen, that suddenly someone can make contact with home and just listen to a familiar voice, but say nothing.

'The girl I spoke to said her name was Lisa Bush and she gave me an address. I told the Gardaí and gave them the number but when the police in Belfast called to the address I'd been given, it turned out to be a false address. Eventually, "Lisa" got rid of the mobile so there's no trace at all now.'

The fact that Lisa denied ringing Michael's parents makes them very suspicious. It would have been easy enough to say 'sorry, wrong number' but she didn't. Then there's the fact that the phone rang three times.

But was it Michael who rang? Or was it just a wrong number. They will always wonder – and hope.

There have been no reported sightings of Michael although all fellow crewmen and passengers on the ferry that night have been questioned.

People wonder how Michael could have left the boat without being seen. Some suggest that he could have travelled off the boat hidden in a truck. Whatever the case and whatever the reason, his family cannot relax until they know what happened to him. 'I'd still love to know what happened to Michael. If someone threw him overboard, if he had an argument with anyone, if they threw him over, we'd still love to know.'

Some would say the trail is now very cold indeed. 'But not in this house it isn't', says his dad, 'we just keep wishing and hoping and praying. And still taking the Valium to keep us going!'

21

James W. Thompson

'Who knows? He may even have children of his own.'

Born 1973, England.
Missing from Dublin since 8 March, 1993.

A shaved head, a pigtail, dreadlocks, Hare Krishna robes – Jamie Thompson changed his appearance many times before his disappearance and may have changed totally again since he went missing while holidaying in Ireland in 1993. That's the dilemma for Jamie's parents Jenny and Michael Thompson when they want to describe their son. Jamie is from Cheltenham, England and he came to Ireland for a holiday in August of that year. He wasn't travelling alone, he had a friend with him and, when the pair reached Dublin, they loved the place. They made friends quickly and settled into a house in Leo Street in the city centre with their new friends.

Jamie kept in contact with his parents and told them he loved Ireland, in particular, he loved the laid-back attitude of the people.

An artistic young man, Jamie was planning to study art in the future and had already been accepted for a course in Gloucester. He had always painted and at one stage was involved in painting designs on leather jackets when that was the height of fashion.

The Christmas before Jamie travelled to Ireland, his parents say he had been depressed, but it wasn't regarded as too serious and they always put bouts like this down to his 'artistic' temperament. 'Until he was 16 or 17, he was very happy, but he had changed as he got older.'

At one stage it looked like Jamie might stay on in Dublin. He discussed this with his parents. He also told them that he felt he had three other options to consider: to join the Hare Krishna movement, to join some new age travellers or to go home.

Eventually Jamie decided to go home to Cheltenham. His arrival date was to be 9 March, 1994. The day before, Jenny rang the house where her son was staying but he wasn't at home. His friends said he had gone out to say goodbye to some other friends but, as far as they knew, his travel plans were still on for the next day. However, Jamie didn't return to the house in Dublin that day or the next. When his friends realised that he hadn't returned, they were concerned, especially when they realised that all his belongings were still in the house. There was no way that Jamie would have travelled and left everything behind him.

His friends went out searching for him, visiting other friends as well as Jamie's usual haunts around Dublin, but there was no sign of him. Jamie has not been seen since, nor has he been in touch with his family or friends.

'To start with', says Jenny, 'you think "he'll come back, he'll get in touch". His friends contacted the Gardaí, my husband went to Dublin but there was no trace of Jamie.'

Even after the trail has gone cold, the family still travel to Dublin, still do interviews with newspapers and radio stations and hope against hope that somebody hears them and has news of Jamie. His parents are adamant that if he doesn't want to be contacted, then that's fine with them. 'We would respect his wishes. All we want to know is that he is well and happy with whatever he has chosen for his life and for him to know that we still love him. Who knows? James may even have children of his own.'

Jamie's appearance changed somewhat after he went to live in Dublin. His friends say he shaved his head and had just a little pigtail at the back. But the old photos show dreadlocks and even a neat crew cut, so it's difficult to know what he looks like now at the age of 30. People who knew the old Jamie may not have recognised the shaved version at the time of his disappearance. This makes it especially difficult for his family, just not knowing if people who knew him before would be able to recognise him now.

Some time after his disappearance there was a reported sighting of him in Hare Krishna robes and, although this has not been verified, his mum feels that he is with the organisation and could be anywhere in the world. The Thompsons have contacted the Hare Krishna movement but they say they have no knowledge of Jamie.

Their 'gut feeling' is that he is still alive, although Jenny admits that she has got into the habit of referring to her son in the past tense and has to correct herself. They also worry that Jamie might not remember their phone number. For two years after his disappearance they were afraid to leave the house in case he rang. Despite missing someone desperately, it is also possible to be very angry with them for going missing, a fact that Jenny is very honest about. She says Jamie's brother Matthew, now aged 33, is angry with his brother for the havoc he has wrought on the family. He recalls that first Christmas when his mum and dad just sat and cried as they waited for the phone to ring.

Jamie's disappearance has also brought about restrictions for his family in Cheltenham. Jenny says they have decided that they cannot move house, nor can they change their telephone number.

Jamie's dad, Michael, an optician, believes that someday his son will just turn up somewhere and he has left instructions with his staff that if any missing persons organisation rings him at work, they are to be put straight through to him. 'I just want to know he is alive and well', he says, 'it's been very traumatic but you learn to live with it as best you can.'

Jamie has now been absent for many family occasions. He wasn't there for his grandmother's death or funeral and several of his cousins have married. His grandad doubts he'll ever see him again. Even in the family, people have stopped talking about Jamie. 'Unless I bring it up, people don't mention him', says Jenny, 'I try not to think too deeply about it but generally nobody mentions him very much. It gets to the stage that you say, what can we do? What can we say?'

22

Imelda Keenan

'I'm still looking everywhere in a crowd.'

Born 24 March, 1971.
Missing from Waterford since 3 January, 1994.

Imelda Keenan is one of a family of nine children. She was reported missing on 3 January, 1994. As the tenth anniversary of her disappearance looms, her family are very anxious to have news of her, to know what happened beyond those last conversations.

Imelda lived in a flat on William Street in Waterford. She is described as a quiet girl who wouldn't go off without telling anyone. When speaking of her disappearance her eldest brother Donal admits 'it was totally out of character'.

Imelda was interested in needlework, sewing and CB radio. CB radio gave her a great interest in making contact with people all over the world. They chatted, they sent on postcards and sometimes they swapped addresses. Obviously, following her disappearance, these contacts became vitally important. Could Imelda have gone to visit someone she met over the radio? All her contacts were followed up after her disappearance but there was no sign of Imelda and no clues there. Her family had also hoped that if she had gone away of her own accord that she would still maintain her interest in radio and would be tempted back onto the air waves but, despite constant monitoring of the waveband, her call sign 'Moonlight Lady' never re-appeared.

On the morning of Monday, 3 January, Imelda told her fiancé, Mark Wall, that she was going down to collect her dole money. It wasn't unusual for Imelda to get up early, but the strange thing is, 3 January was a bank holiday and the dole office was closed. She should have collected her dole the previous Friday, but the family later discovered it had never been collected. However, this wasn't the only strange thing about that week. Her family later discovered that Imelda hadn't even opened her Christmas presents. They were still in her flat intact in their gift wrapping with cards of seasonal greetings.

On the day she left home, Imelda took nothing with her. It wasn't a day to be out and about in the city as the quays were partly flooded. Mark said she was always home before dark and he became concerned when she didn't return home. Imelda was never seen again.

Her eldest brother, Ned, lived just down the road and he and Imelda were close friends. He was something of a father figure to his youngest sister. Imelda helped to care for Ned's children, Edward and Richard, collecting them from school and taking them to the park to play. They are now grown up and they miss their aunt a lot but, as Donal points out, Imelda was 22 when she disappeared and 'it's not a crime to go missing'. He has been told by the experts that after 10 days away, it gets a bit harder to return home and after two years it becomes very hard indeed. As time passes it becomes almost impossible.

Donal remembers the days after she went missing as 'total turmoil for the family. We were afraid to answer the phone or the door and got a start if we saw a garda car on the street. We dreaded late-night phone calls in case it was bad news.' They kept busy because 'there was always some new thing to be chasing. We watched the canal, we searched the woods, and we went to clairvoyants. I drove my sisters to one clairvoyant who told them "she'll never walk back through your door again". Another said "she passed not far from here on a train".' Another told Imelda's sister, Liz, that she was in heaven with her father (who had died in 1988) and that she loved her mother.

The family have liaised with Gardaí, put up posters and followed up on sightings. 'People are trying to give you hope, they don't lie about the sightings but they want to help and a glimpse of somebody who looks like the missing person can often result in a "sighting", especially among young people, so many of them do indeed look the same. They wear the same type of clothes, have the same type of hairstyles and do lead complete strangers to think they've spotted someone. There really weren't any sightings of Imelda though', says Donal.

This 'false sightings syndrome', as one family described it, is still something that the families are very grateful for. It means that ordinary people out there are keeping an eye out, are alert for someone who may be in trouble and have heeded the appeals for help. In fairness, some families have experienced the malicious call, the hoax caller, but they are in the minority. Some of the sightings of other missing persons have turned out to be positive, perhaps moving the search on a little bit or eliminating certain areas of investigation.

The Keenans are a very close family. 'Mum has the family behind her', Donal says. They are adamant that Imelda will not be declared 'dead' despite the fact that she has been missing for more than the statutory seven years, 'it would not be right', they say. They have considered the possibility that she may have been murdered, but can't think of either a motive or a place where it might have happened.

Imelda's mother, Elizabeth, has another theory. She believes that her daughter may have been sucked into a cult. 'She was a religious type of person, as a child she played as a nun and told us she'd love to be a teaching nun when she grew up. The only place you can go with only the clothes on your back is into a cult where there's no contact with the outside world, no photos, no reminders of home.'

Things have moved on in the Keenan family. There have been deaths and marriages and births. But Imelda is remembered and there are family videos to keep her memory alive for a younger generation. Elizabeth believes that Imelda is still alive but 'I'd like to know one way or the other', she says, 'I went to Lourdes for her and asked Our Lady and St. Bernadette and the Blessed Virgin – whose birthday I share – to help. I told the Blessed Virgin that her son knows where my baby is. One way or another, I'd like to find Imelda before I go.'

The family feel that there was something on Imelda's mind for a month or so before her disappearance. Mark told Ned he was worried about her, that he couldn't get through to her and, although she loved a cuppa and a cigarette, he knew something was wrong when he found her sitting up drinking tea and smoking at four o'clock in the morning.

Ned brought her out to play pool and to have a chat and found a big change from the jolly person she usually was. 'She had no laugh in her', he told his mother and when he asked her what was on her mind, Imelda told him, 'Ah, I got this old feeling before Ned and it passed over and it'll pass over this time again.' Before he left her, Ned made her promise him that if she didn't feel well she would visit the doctor and Imelda agreed. That was the last time Ned saw his sister.

Imelda was engaged to Mark for five years, but was in no hurry to get married. When the couple announced their engagement Elizabeth didn't approve because her daughter was only 17. But Imelda allayed her fears pointing out that 'you can be engaged for years and can change your mind and not get married'. She told her mother that she would still be engaged when she celebrated her 21st birthday (as indeed she was), and said she understood the difference between an engagement ring and a wedding ring.

Imelda loved animals and kept a cat and three goldfish, named Moby, Toby and Dick. The pets are long gone but Elizabeth still keeps the cuddly toys, the roomful of photos and Imelda's glasses. It's hard for the family to realise that Imelda has been missing for ten years. 'I'm still looking everywhere in a crowd for a 23-year-old girl and she is 33 now. I still shed tears for her', says Elizabeth.

23

Eva Brennan

'We were like the seven little Indians.'

Born 15 July, 1953.
Missing from Terenure, Dublin since 25 July, 1993.

On Sunday, 25 July, 1993, Eva Brennan left her family home in Terenure. She has not been seen since.

Eva was 39 at the time, disappearing 10 days before her 40th birthday. It was a bank holiday weekend and, as was her habit of a Sunday, Eva, who lived down the road in Rathgar, came to her parents' house in Terenure for Sunday lunch. It was a typical family Sunday and Eva's brothers were up in the house as well, relaxing and chatting before lunch. It was a normal day characterised by the usual family atmosphere.

Eva wasn't in the best of form, like everyone she had her off days, and there was no more perfect environment in which to be cranky than around the family. In an irritable mood she wandered into the kitchen and went over to the oven, opened the oven door to have a look inside and see what her mum had cooking. 'Not fecking lamb again', she moaned as she walked into her brothers in the living room. Siblings are the worst people to complain to as they never have any sympathy for a family member's moaning and Eva's brother told her, reasonably, if she wasn't happy with the menu she didn't have to stay. The mood that Eva was in that day, she decided to take him at his word and she walked out the door. That was the last time Eva was ever seen.

Eva's sister, Colette McCann, says she has to laugh when she recalls the simple little incident that Sunday at her parents' house. 'There was nothing unusual about it. There were seven children in the family. We were all incredibly close and inevitably, as in all big families, one or other of us was always grumbling at each other. There was nothing to worry about. We left Eva to get on with it.'

The family didn't worry, expecting Eva to drop in over the next day or two. 'Most days Eva came up to Mum's for lunch.' When the family had still heard nothing from Eva two days later, the following Tuesday, they wondered whether something was up. On Tuesday evening her Dad suggested that they pop down to Eva's house in Rathgar to see if she was around. After ringing the doorbell a couple of times, and still receiving no reply on the intercom, they feared something could be wrong.

The family alerted a barman they knew who worked in a pub across the road and he came over to help them. Between them they broke the window of Eva's house and gained entry. The house was completely silent. Eva was not there. There were no signs of a disturbance, everything was exactly as it always was. The Sunday she had left her parents' house, Eva had been wearing a jacket, which they found in her apartment, indicating that she had been home, however, whether she stayed in or went out after that remains a mystery. 'We figure she went back home and then went out somewhere. I don't know. Eva never travelled far. She lived on the Templeogue Road and stayed very much in the Templeogue/Rathgar area.' The family later discovered that she hadn't taken a change of clothes, any extra money or her passport. It did not look like she had been planning to go away and she certainly hadn't told anyone of any plans to go away.

Eva's sister, Colette, who was supposed to be going away that week, received a call from her father to say that her sister was missing and the police had been called in. Colette was shocked by the news and cancelled her plans to go away. Although stunned, she was also immediately conscious that she couldn't get caught up in the emotion of the situation, as she would be of no help to anyone that way. 'I immediately realised someone had to take charge. I moved into my parents' home straight away.'

As the reality of the situation began to hit the family, everyone was confused and bewildered and Colette knew that someone had to keep a clear head and be realistic about what needed to be done to search for Eva. Colette saw that she would have to put her emotions on hold and take a practical approach. She took over the search and began to explore every avenue starting, with the help of other family members, with contacting everyone who knew Eva, making endless phone calls to see if there was any lead they could follow. It was a very strange situation – Eva had vanished without trace, seemingly out of the blue. In order that people would know that she was missing, and indeed know what she looked like, the family put posters up everywhere they could.

Colette also had to take on the huge task of giving countless interviews to the press, which was of vital importance in order to alert as many people as possible to Eva's disappearance. She was constantly giving interviews to reporters for newspapers, radio and magazines in an effort to get the information out quickly to as many places as possible.

The members of the Brennan family also went out themselves scouring the area for any sign of Eva. Everybody in the family is able to drive and they set out in their cars, searching the surrounding area for hours on end, looking for any sign of her. 'Rathgar is a crossroads

– we went in every direction.' The family contacted everyone, including friends and other people who knew Eva, but the search turned up nothing. Nobody had seen or heard anything of Eva since that Sunday at her parents' home. She seemed to have literally vanished. There wasn't even the option of tracking her through a mobile phone. Mobile phones weren't as much the norm in 1993 and Eva did not have one.

Colette McCann is 100 per cent convinced that Eva is dead.

'I felt it straight away, the moment I heard she was missing. Something sinister was happening at the time. Eight women disappeared suddenly in a very short space of time. Eva went missing 12 weeks after Annie McCarrick. She went missing from Rathgar; Annie went missing from near the same area. She went missing the same way the others went missing, suddenly and with no explanation. To go so totally – eight of them without trace of any of them – there was something very strange going on in that period. By the weekend following her disappearance, I knew she wasn't coming home. I knew something was seriously wrong.'

The Brennan family doesn't know what happened to Eva. People, naturally, hear her story and come up with all kinds of theories that seem logical to them.

'People will always speculate. I know Eva did not commit suicide. She had suffered from depression, which we decided to make public when Eva went missing. We didn't want it to come out at a later stage and people jumping to all sorts of conclusions. We've all suffered from not being in top form on occasions. For the past three to four years Eva was grand. People can have whatever theories they want. The newspapers had plenty to make of it at the time. My belief is the same as I had at the beginning, something horrible happened to Eva. She was murdered. I am convinced she is dead. It was not in her nature – or any of the family's nature – to go off and say nothing. One of us would always be over at my parents' house. I'd go over Tuesdays and Thursdays, Robert on Tuesdays and Fridays. Eva was always around at my parents' or one of our houses. You know your own, if Eva was alive she wouldn't have hurt Mum and Dad.'

The effect of Eva's disappearance has obviously been devastating for the Brennan family. Colette is sure her parents knew from the beginning that Eva was dead, but could not bring themselves to admit it for reasons that we can all understand. Colette feels the males in the family found it particularly hard to accept. 'I don't think the boys or Dad believed Eva was dead. What father or brother wants to accept that their daughter or sister was brutally raped or murdered? The boys and Dad were bewildered.' Eva's mother, Eileen Brennan, didn't leave the house for four years following Eva's disappearance. A mother's worst nightmare had come true – the daughter she had given birth to, whom she had believed would always be there, long after she passed on, was gone – they did not know where she was, whether she was in danger, in need of help, alive or dead.

Eileen pleaded with Colette to stop doing interviews with the press as she couldn't face the trauma of opening up the papers and seeing her missing daughter staring out at her. It was an unusual sensation. 'I told Mum I had to keep doing interviews. If I stopped, Eva would have no voice. Eva has to have a voice.'

The Brennan children managed to persuade their father to go racing as he always had done. They wanted their parents to try and continue with their lives, despite the torture of knowing that their daughter was out there somewhere, but not knowing where. Colette's sister, Eileen, and brother, Paul, stood behind her in her endless efforts to find out what happened to Eva. The three struggled to keep their sanity for Eva's sake, for the sake of the family. 'Myself, Eileen and Paul were like the three musketeers. We went everywhere together in search of Eva. We never stopped. Eva's disappearance hurt people and affected us all in different ways. The three of us tried to rationalise.'

It can be very difficult for families of missing people to talk about their loved one as just the mention of their name brings to mind all the fears and worries about what could have happened to them. It was a long time before the Brennans were comfortable discussing Eva. 'Now, we can talk about her. After ten years I'm finally grieving – I didn't have the time before. I'm sadder now. It's very difficult for Mum, you don't have seven children and expect one of them to go missing but we do talk about Eva, me and Mum.'

At the time of speaking to Colette she said there is not even one per cent of her that believes Eva is alive. Colette turned down an interview on a Dublin radio station in 2003, just saying, 'There's no point.' The day she was asked to do the interview had been particularly difficult for Colette. She was organising with Coillte to have a bench commissioned and placed in the graveyard where her father was buried, to mark the tenth anniversary of Eva's disappearance. 'Daddy was 81 when he died. He got stomach cancer in November 2000 and died on the 28 February, 2001, he went very fast. I believe Eva is with my father in heaven. Eva's disappearance destroyed my father, men are not able to accept it.'

There is a particularly nice memory Colette has of her father's funeral: 'I remember Daddy's funeral, there were a lot of people at it. A friend of ours was telling us she was talking to a stranger at the bus stop that day who said, "Is that Davy Brennan whose daughter went missing? I used to sit beside her in the church for her lovely smile and shaking her hand. She was a good, kind person".'

Only now can Colette McCann really grieve for her sister, Eva. Organising the bench for Eva finally gave Colette a point of closure. She undertook the bench project by herself. 'The others were happy for me to do it and will go up to it when they are ready. It was a very peculiar feeling when I put the bench up. It hurt, I was very upset.' The Brennans had a mass said for Eva, but didn't have a memorial service, as that would be too final they felt, since they hadn't found a body. Although a person can be declared dead after they have been missing for seven years, the family hasn't declared her officially dead. 'We did talk about putting her on the headstone with Dad. What we finally decided was to inscribe "in loving memory of Eva Brennan, missing since 25 July, 1993" on the bench.'

The family will never get over Eva's disappearance, but have realised for everyone's sake that they have to get on with life. 'You don't get over it.' Colette thinks of her younger sister every day, in a good way. 'She was a pain in the ass sometimes', she laughs, 'she was next to me in age and used to rob my clothes and make-up. She was a very nice person, normal like the rest of us.' All seven siblings in the large Brennan family always got on like a house on fire. She remembers fondly how they used to terrorise the neighbours when they were children: 'We were like the seven little Indians, rampaging around the area, robbing orchards and the like when we were kids. The seven of us – Pete, myself, Eva, David, Eileen, Robert and Paul – were mad. We were the mad Brennans.'

Eva didn't work, the Brennan boys followed their father into the pub business while the girls did bits and bobs. 'We girls didn't have to work, Dad spoiled us rotten.' Eva had boyfriends on and off, but never married. 'She was a good kind person. She didn't have kids. She would always be there at Christmas and birthdays with presents for my kids. I'm sure she would have loved to have been married.' Eva also went to prayer meetings. 'She'd joke to Eileen and myself, and say, "I was put on this earth to pray for you heathens." She had a dry wit, a great sense of humour. I miss Eva, I miss my sister. I miss her smile. What none of us will ever forget about Eva is her smile. She had a fantastic smile.'

The Brennans no longer expect Eva to walk through the door. The family believes she is at peace. 'I'd love to give her a decent burial.' Colette personally wants to find Eva's body, 'I'd love to bury her with Dad. It's not fair that she's maybe lying somewhere.' Colette has no desire to punish somebody for Eva's disappearance: 'I'm not interested in catching anyone for it. I don't want to hate someone for it. She is happier where she is, in heaven. It's unimportant who did something to her; it makes no difference except for him. We all have to face up to our conscience. I don't know whether it's the day of judgement or what – I'm not deeply religious myself. The only thing that does worry me is that in 20 or 30 years time my kids will be left with the task of finding her body.'

Like many of the families of missing people, the Brennans were disappointed by the reaction of the Gardaí when Eva went missing. 'The police didn't seem to do a lot. I don't think they looked for her at all. There was no search conducted on their part as far as I know. They didn't even ask for her address books until three years after she disappeared. Of course if they could prove to me that they did conduct a search now, I'd believe it. My impression is that the budget was blown on the search for Annie McCarrick.

'The first thing I feel the police should have done was check the buses on the routes in the area, I don't know whether they did that. The first thing you should do when someone goes missing is put up a photo so people know what to look out for, but I don't see it being done. We weren't informed of any steps being taken to search for Eva.' This issue comes up over and over again when someone goes missing. No one expects a family member to go missing and most haven't an idea where to begin the search when it happens. Those who are left behind are also in no fit state of mind to regard the matter logically. This is where they need professionals to step in, especially as speed is of the essence.

Colette says that after her family conducted a search for two years, they came up with a list of things you do when someone goes missing. 'The police asked me for a copy of it,' says Colette.

'Only after Eva had been missing for nine years, did I realise that they had a liaison officer for families of missing people. I had never heard from anyone. We did everything ourselves. We even got a private detective, who was useless. We still haven't received written reports from him.'

The main support lies in the network of parents and families of missing people. Those who have had the experience of a loved one going missing can identify with other families and will do anything to help out. They can offer a huge amount of advice in terms of what to do when carrying out a search as they have first-hand experience of what does and does not work. 'We are all here trying to help each other and if I can be of any help to others, I would be very happy to talk to families who have had someone go missing.'

Eva's family are determined to keep her memory very much alive. Her siblings make sure that their children know who Eva is. 'We have pictures up of her. Years ago it was teaching the children but now it's just normal conversation.' Colette laughs: 'They're fed up hearing about Eva. We have come to terms with it. It has happened and there's no point in being all funny about it.'

Colette has always tried to keep things as normal as possible in her home. She made sure to conduct research and do interviews with the press while her children were at school, maintaining a normal family atmosphere when the children were at home. Inevitably, Colette and her family are a lot more conscious of the dangers out there than most families, however she is determined not to smother her children or allow it to have an adverse effect on her family.

'I do tell my daughter to be careful. Obviously we'd be more aware than others that things like this do actually happen. I warn her not to drink too much when she goes out and remind her to make sure to always carry a mobile phone, like any mother would, but you have to keep things normal for the kids. I don't want to be over-protective and I think my daughter has grown up fine.'

After all these years, Colette says she would like to know her sister's fate after she left the family home on that Sunday of the Bank Holiday weekend: 'I suppose I do want to know what happened to Eva. It's a natural curiosity. In one sense I want to know it all, just to tell me why, but I don't want to hate. You can go a lot of ways; you can be bitter or try to lead your life, for your own sake, for your children's sake and just hope to be a better person for it. There are a couple of ways you can think. You can lose your normal life or figure out a way of dealing with it.'

'You have to fight to maintain normality. I will always remember the good old days with Eva but you do have to keep going, especially when you have a family and children. You can have all these things or you can have nothing.

'It's such a mystery, most peculiar to have a sister "just gone", "just vanished". The terrible thing is, she's gone but she's not gone. She is not officially dead. I miss her', Colette reflects sadly, 'I miss her for being my sister. I miss her smile.'

Things to Do When Someone Goes Missing (compiled by Colette McCann)

1. Report the person missing.
2. Talk to family and friends. Maybe the person is staying with someone or someone has seen them or has information that may provide clues.
3. Ring the Missing Persons Helpline.
4. Print posters as soon as possible. Getting the message out that a person has gone missing is useless if no one knows what the person looks like.
5. Contact the press and insist that they distribute pictures.
6. Contact television and radio stations.
7. Check the phone. Find out details of the last calls the person made on their mobile or house phone. Find out who they talked to last.
8. Check their e-mail. See if there are any e-mails from the missing person.
9. Check their bank account. Are they withdrawing money?
10. Check if their passport has been taken.
11. Check their house or where they are staying to see if anything is missing, if anything is out of place, or if there is any sign of disorder.

12. Check if the person's personal belongings are in the place they should be. Is anything missing?
13. Check for fingerprints immediately. If you leave it for too long, there will be too many other prints from the police and people searching for clues.
14. Check bus routes and public transport. Talk to bus drivers and people who take the same bus every day, especially people who know the missing person.
15. Check the Internet. Look for helpful Missing Persons websites and register the person as missing.
16. Ask the police to keep in contact. It is very important to know what is going on.
17. Consider DNA testing and test the family immediately, especially the parents. You never know when this may be needed.
18. Check CCTV cameras from the area around where the person went missing.
19. Don't be put off. You know your own. This is very important – family members know the missing person best. The police may say 'They'll be back' or there could be misleading newspaper reports, but at the end of the day, you know the person missing.
20. Be kind to yourself. This is very important. When a loved one goes missing, everyone forgets to do everything – they forget to eat and drink. It is very important to keep your sanity by continuing with your hobbies, continuing to go out, getting on with your life. A lot of people tend to stay in and retreat into themselves.

24

Michelle McCormick

'I would stay with her for a little while and bury her in a nice little place where Leona could visit.'

Born 28 March, 1970.
Missing from Owenahincha Holiday Park, Cork since 10 July, 1993.

This is the story of a 23-year-old Cork woman, Michelle McCormick, presumed dead, whose body has never been found.

Michelle's mother, Kathleen, and Thomas Linehan were brother and sister and both families grieved when Michelle disappeared in 1993, eight years before her uncle went missing.

You can read Thomas' story in Chapter 29.

Michelle is described by her mother, Kathleen, as 'always very happy and bubbly. She liked to make us laugh, she was very kind and very soft hearted'. She worked in the catering business, in bars and in restaurants but she wasn't working at the time of her disappearance as she was caring for her 16-month-old daughter, Leona.

Michelle was the middle child in the family with three brothers, Gerry, Adrian and Tony, and two sisters, Jacqueline and Donna. They are now aged from 25 to 40. Their father died when they were very young but Kathleen has a partner, Joe Murphy, who has done enormous work in the search for Michelle. Kathleen says Joe has 'been my rock through all of this'.

It should have been a very happy time for the family. Michelle and her partner and Leona were on holiday at Owenahincha Holiday Park in West Cork when she disappeared. Also on the holiday were a couple of her siblings. They all got on very well and were happy to holiday together, but something happened in Owenahincha. Nobody knows exactly what did happen but Michelle disappeared from the lives of her family. It is now believed she was murdered although a body has never been found.

On the Saturday night, the family arrived back in Mayfield with Leona and told Kathleen that Michelle had gone missing, that she hadn't been seen since the early hours of the previous Monday morning.

Kathleen knew the news was bad from the moment she took in her granddaughter. 'I knew from the start that something terrible had happened to Michelle, I can't explain it, it was just something I felt. The first few years after she went missing were total blackness, it was a question of just putting one foot in front of the other. Only for Leona I wouldn't have got up out of bed in the mornings, I am so lucky to have her with me.'

The fact that Michelle was missing for almost a week before Gardaí were brought in on the case made it more difficult to collect evidence of her last movements. Searches were organised and Kathleen pays tribute to her family, friends and neighbours who headed off to West Cork to look for Michelle. They put in long days and nights scouring the area where Michelle was last seen, the places she had visited on that fateful holiday and talking to local people who might have seen something unusual. Kathleen's nephew, David Linehan, brought in sub aqua divers, but they found nothing.

This is a very complicated case because, some years later, a man, confessed to Michelle's murder, was charged and the trial got underway. However, the trial collapsed when the judge directed the jury to find the defendant not guilty because certain aspects of the evidence were found to be inadmissible.

Usually a trial doesn't take place without a body. However, a trial is possible if someone confesses to the murder which is what happened in this case. The trial was based on a confession but collapsed when this confession was later withdrawn.

In 1977, a conviction was secured for the murder of Captain Robert Nairic, a British SAS Captain, despite the fact that his body was never found. A confession, along with circumstantial evidence, proved sufficient. Superintendent John Farrelly of An Garda Síochána admits, however, that it is extremely difficult to secure a conviction without the discovery of the victim's body.

The collapse of the trial left Michelle's family devastated. 'That was the one thing that kept us going over the years', says Kathleen, 'the thought of getting justice.'

Kathleen says there is no question of her daughter being found alive, 'I know she's not coming back, but I really do want to find her, to have some closure on her life'.

Kathleen still reacts with shock every time a body is found somewhere. The first thought is that it might be Michelle, 'In the beginning my heart would be jumping and it's still a little bit like that.'

Today Kathleen's wish is just to find her daughter's body. 'I'd like to find her, to stay with her for a little while and bury her in a nice little place where Leona could visit her. Leona was only 16 months old when her Mum disappeared and she has kept me going.' Kathleen has raised Leona, who is now 11, and has told her all she knows about Michelle's disappearance and probable death.

Today there are 22 grandchildren in the family and there is a great sadness that a part of this big happy family is missing from the picture. But Kathleen has her strong memories of her daughter, 'Michelle was so wonderful to me', she says, 'she was a beautiful girl, small and petite, a good friend and a great mother'.

25

Annie McCarrick

'They are not angry with the Irish as a race; they know Annie was happy here.'

Missing from Dublin since 26 March, 1993.

The case of the young American woman who fell in love with Ireland, studied and lived here for three years, and who went missing without trace in the Wicklow Mountains has baffled the Gardaí for the past number of years.

From time to time visitors have gone missing in this country, but nothing gripped the nation as did the search for Annie McCarrick. She first visited Ireland when she was 20 years old and her initial love of the country and its people led to her decision to study here. She spent three years studying at both St. Patrick's Teacher Training College in Dublin and at Maynooth College. During her student years she even spent the summer travelling and working with her Irish friends. There were also strong Irish connections on both sides of her family, family friendships with Irish people living in New York and a strong sense from Annie that she was at home here, that she belonged. She had made many friends in Ireland but they could throw no light on her disappearance.

At the time of her disappearance, Annie was living in Sandymount in Dublin and had a job in a restaurant in the city. Annie loved the countryside so it wasn't considered in any way strange that she might have gone for a long walk on 26 March, 1993, the day she disappeared. She was seen taking a bus from Ranelagh in Dublin towards Enniskerry in Co. Wicklow. She had called a friend earlier in the day and asked her if she wanted to go walking in Wicklow but her friend declined because she was recovering from a foot injury. So Annie set off alone shortly after three o'clock on the Friday afternoon.

There was no sign that she hadn't intended to return. She had invited two friends over for dinner the following day and had bought some of the ingredients for the meal. She had chatted to a friend on the phone the previous evening and she was looking forward to a visit from her mother a week later. Her mother, Nancy, visited Annie about once a year in the springtime. They were great friends and Annie went to a lot of trouble to make sure Nancy enjoyed her stay. After her disappearance, gardaí found theatre tickets in her apartment, bought with her mother's visit in mind. Also, none of the people she had spoken to thought there was anything unusual about those last conversations.

There were a number of sightings of Annie on the day of her disappearance. She was seen as she left her apartment, as she almost missed her first bus, the 18, when the driver slowed to wait for her, and as she travelled on a second bus, the 44, in the direction of Co. Wicklow. A woman who knew Annie was actually at the same bus stop for the 44 but was ahead of her in the queue. It was a very definite sighting because this woman had worked in a restaurant with Annie only a month earlier and would not have been mistaken. When the bus arrived the woman sat downstairs but Annie went upstairs, so the two never actually got a chance to chat. The incident was most useful to the Gardaí as it confirmed that Annie had at least travelled some way towards Co. Wicklow.

Annie's movements earlier in the day were also well documented. She had spoken to her two flatmates before they left for a weekend away. Later, Annie went shopping in Sandymount and visited the Allied Irish Bank branch, which caught her on CCTV.

However, once she left her home shortly after three o'clock that afternoon, no one knows exactly where Annie went walking, although it may have been close to the village of Enniskerry. That evening, there was another possible sighting of Annie, this time in Johnny Fox's Pub, on the fringes of the Dublin Mountains.

If it was Annie, how did she get there? She could have walked or she could have hitched, but with whom? Could she have bumped into someone she knew? Had she arranged to meet a friend? These are the questions that the Gardaí have been seeking answers for over the years.

People who remembered seeing Annie in the pub said she was in the company of a man, but this man has never been traced despite appeals, reconstructions and her family hiring a private investigator. If, indeed, it was Annie in the pub that evening, then it is very strange that the man with her has never come forward, and this leads detectives to believe that he must have something to hide.

Many people believe that Annie McCarrick was murdered on the day she went missing. She has been included in that group of women whose disappearances were investigated as part of Operation Trace in the search for a possible serial killer.

The other thing to be considered is that when Annie arrived in Enniskerry, there was little daylight left. She couldn't have gone for a particularly long walk.

There may have been another sighting of her in the post office in the village, as a young woman who looked like Annie bought stamps there.

Annie's friends raised the alarm when she didn't turn up for work and her flatmates hadn't heard from her. One of them rang her mother, Nancy, in Long Island and she immediately took a flight to Dublin, with her husband following a short time later. Other family members also flew over to help in the search and Annie's parents remained in Ireland for two months. Over the years, they have returned many times, they have met with the gardaí investigating the case and have been given updates on the search. They have stood by the phone too many times hoping for news of their daughter, only to have their hopes cruelly dashed.

Nancy was met at the airport the next morning by her daughter's friend, Hilary Brady. It was Hilary and his fiancée who had been invited to Annie's apartment for dinner the night after she disappeared, but when they arrived as planned there was no answer. Hilary and his family had known Annie for about five years and he reasoned that it was totally out of character for Annie to cancel an arrangement without letting them know. Hilary hadn't got Annie's phone number with him, so he rang Annie's mother in New York for the number. He rang and rang the number he was given but there was no reply.

As soon as Nancy arrived in Dublin, she and Hilary went to the gardaí in Irishtown to report Annie as a missing person. A huge search was launched together with back up media coverage, but nothing was ever found of Annie. The mountain roads between Enniskerry and Johnny Fox's pub were searched meticulously, there were investigative digs in some of the forests and, each summer, when the sun and wind dried out the bogs, walkers kept watch for anything strange which might emerge from the turf.

Although a popular tourist area, this mountainous region between Dublin and Wicklow is a very lonely place. In March there are few day-trippers and walkers and it gets dark very early, optimum conditions for someone trying to conceal a body. The mountains themselves are criss-crossed with turf paths and boreens, many of which can take a car for a half-mile or so up into the mountains. Then there are the lakes, deep and dark and difficult to reach from a main road. The possibilities for getting rid of a body were endless.

Gardaí were also conscious that the area had been used for the disposal of other bodies in the past. The body of Patricia Doherty was found there in 1992 and also, four years earlier, that of Antoinette Smith. Gardaí interviewed hundreds of people, walkers, locals and those who had been in Johnnie Fox's pub that evening. Annie was fond of traditional Irish music and may even have planned to end her day at the pub listening to music. If this were the case, then the search for her abductor might focus on the journey back to Dublin and the home Annie never saw again.

Following the extensive publicity on the case, many people came forward with suggestions and possible sightings. One of these was a young nurse who told gardaí that she had been walking in an area of the Dublin Mountains with her dog about a month after Annie disappeared. The dog ran ahead of her to a clearing in woodland and she heard something fall. When she got there she realised that her dog had knocked something over which had been standing against a tree trunk. It turned out to be a spade, wrapped in black plastic bags. This nurse said she felt there was something very unpleasant about the clearing. Then she got a very bad smell and she said that, as a nurse, she knew the smell of decaying flesh. She left the area and alerted the Gardaí.

She accompanied them back to where the spade had been found and they began a search of the area. In the course of that search, gardaí found a holdall in a ditch which contained the body of a large dog. The smell was attributed to the dog and the search ended. However, the presence of a wrapped spade left behind in a woodland has never been explained. To this day, the nurse believes that the area should have been searched more widely and thoroughly and that perhaps the Gardaí gave up too soon when they found the dog in the sports bag.

Perhaps the most bizarre investigation into the disappearance of Annie McCarrick, however, was the digging up of a pet cemetery at Kilmolin, outside Enniskerry in 1997. The dig came about after a chance remark to a detective that two young men had buried what they claimed was a dog in a very large box in the cemetery one winter evening shortly after Annie disappeared. The owner of the cemetery, which caters for small pets such as dogs, cats and rabbits, had told them where they should bury the dog and offered assistance, but they were adamant they would do the job themselves. They had also opted for a 'trench' form of burial rather than an individual plot. The trench was already dug out with a mechanical digger and the pets were placed in a section of the trench, with the particular stretch being filled in immediately. Therefore, because of the nature of these burials it would be impossible to pinpoint exactly where a particular animal had been buried. The cemetery also has individual plots, but on the day these young men called to bury their dog, they chose to use the trench.

After initial investigations, it was decided to dig up the pet cemetery. This was a huge operation, made difficult by the sheer volume of burials over the years as well as the lack of a method of recording specific information in the early years of the cemetery's operation. Annie's parents were told the dig was going to take place and were kept informed throughout. If Annie's remains had been found in the cemetery, then they were going to travel to Ireland immediately.

On 16 June, amid much secrecy, a large contingent of forensic scientists moved into the cemetery and started to sift through the graves. Initially it was done by hand, then they brought in a small mechanical digger to assist. They tried to keep the dig secret but by mid-morning it was well publicised in the media. This had the effect of alerting dozens of pet owners who arrived at the gates to query the disturbance of their pets' graves. Many of these people had invested time, effort and love in their pets' last resting place. Some had purchased expensive marble stones to put on the graves and, although they supported the search for the missing American woman, they resented the disturbance of the graves.

The gardaí used a video camera to film the graves before they dug them up to make certain that all the headstones would be replaced exactly as they were. One of the more unpleasant aspects of the dig was the fact that many of the pet owners had actually buried their animals in sealed plastic bags so that, when they decomposed, the remains couldn't return to the earth but rotted inside the bag. The fumes made the detective's job almost unbearable at times.

The dig went on for two days. The ownership of the cemetery had changed in the meantime and the new owners were bemused by what was happening just yards from their home, but they co-operated totally with the gardaí, explaining as best they could the previous burial pattern in the cemetery.

A breakthrough came after a report on the Pat Kenny show about the dig, in which I told the story of the two young men and the large wooden box. Almost immediately, two brothers got in touch with the show and with the Gardaí to say that it was them who had buried the dog. They travelled to the cemetery and explained to gardaí there that the family pet – a very large dog – had died, and a friend of their mothers, who was a cabinet maker, had offered to make a coffin for the dog. However, he overestimated the size of the dog and made a very large wooden box, which was far too big for the dead animal. This was part of the reason that they had told the proprietor they would bury it themselves.

Arriving at the cemetery, the brothers took gardaí to the spot where they remembered burying the dog. After a short time digging, the large wooden box was uncovered. However, in the slim hope that something else was contained inside, gardaí were given a break before returning to deal with whatever lay in the box. A corner of the box was forced open and, sure enough, it was the last resting place of a huge dog. Gardaí were disappointed but, at the same time, relieved that Annie hadn't been buried in Kilmolin. The gardaí then got down to the job of replacing all the pet headstones and getting the graves in order before their anxious owners returned to check on them.

Searching

The search for Annie goes on. Her parents have made follow-up trips to Ireland but no further information has ever been uncovered. Annie made many good friends in Ireland and they too have been devastated by her loss. Today her family accept that Annie was murdered and that, because of the delay in realising she was missing, her abductor had about 48 hours head start on the Gardaí and thus plenty of time to conceal her body.

The other strange thing about Annie's disappearance was that there was never a prime suspect. In many of the other cases of missing women, family and friends will name people they have their own suspicions about. In towns and villages names are spoken in pubs and among friends but in Annie's case, there was nobody.

The hope remains that some day Annie's remains will surface somewhere. Her parents, now divorced, continue to hope that their only child will be found. They are not angry with the Irish as a race, they know that Annie was happy here, but they need some closure on one of the most baffling mysteries among the disappeared.

26

Joseph Kelly

'I think Joseph is up in heaven.'

Missing from Castlebar, Co. Mayo since 13 November, 1992.

Michael and Christina Kelly from Newport, Co. Mayo wake up each morning determined to get on with their lives, and they struggle to make each day as normal as possible, because each day dawns bringing with it a terrible burden. This November marks the 11th anniversary of the disappearance of their son, Joseph Kelly.

On the 13 November, 1992, Joseph Kelly went missing from St. Teresa's hospital in Castlebar, Co. Mayo. He was 19 years old at the time. His father Michael had dropped him off at the hospital that morning as he usually did, expecting to pick him up from the bus stop later. Joseph usually took the bus home to his parents' house in the evening and his father would meet him there, but he was not on the bus that evening.

Michael received a phone call from St. Teresa's hospital telling him that Joseph had disappeared from the hospital that afternoon and could not be found. The hospital had contacted the police and all units were alerted to look out for him.

On receiving the call from the hospital, Michael and Christina were immediately worried. This was not the first time Joseph had gone missing. He suffered from bi-polar disorder and had to go to the hospital for treatment every day. But every other time Joseph had gone missing he had turned up within a couple of hours. This time, after a few hours passed, Joseph was still missing. As the evening passed and there was still no sign of him, his parents were extremely concerned.

The family launched their own search for Joseph. Family and friends were contacted to take part, but it was very difficult to know how to go about it. The family were very distressed and it took a lot to approach the search calmly and with a clear head. Michael wondered whether Joseph had gone to a friend's house, and so he began to make phone calls: 'We didn't know where to start.'

The phone calls led to nothing, no one had seen Joseph. The night approached and he was still missing. The police were on the lookout, but it appeared that he had literally vanished into thin air. The first thing the family did was get a photo of Joseph and blow it up into a poster. They then made endless copies. They began the search in the local area, putting up posters and searching the streets, asking everyone whether they had seen him. Michael spent many sleepless nights looking for his son. As the days passed and there was no word of Joseph, Michael knew they had to consider the possibility that something serious could have happened to Joseph. The Clew Bay sub aqua diving club put themselves at the family's disposal and searched the rivers and lakes looking for him, but still they found nothing.

As the days turned into weeks, the family became more and more concerned. They couldn't understand where Joseph had got to. Michael was desperate to find his son and determined to explore every avenue. They scoured the local area and their search took them through the whole of County Mayo. They didn't leave a stone unturned. 'We searched the whole county, from Westport to Partry to Belmullet.' Then there was news of a possible sighting of him on Achill island. Michael set out for Achill immediately. 'I went to the island and stayed there for a few days. I travelled around the whole of Achill looking everywhere for Joseph, but there was no sign of him at all.' Michael finally left the island. It is very easy to mistake someone for a missing person. If you don't know the person, you only have a picture to go on and there are often an endless number of people who seem to resemble the face from the poster.

The Clew Bay sub aqua team stuck with the search, exploring all possible waterways. They dived the river in Partry, they also dived Lough Mask and Ballyglass. When they were met with nothing but dead ends in Mayo, Michael decided to continue the search in Dublin, where he got together with a garda friend. Together, they searched night and day. They went to every possible place they felt he could be. They visited hostels for homeless people, in the hope that one of the residents might turn out to be the missing Joseph. They also walked street after street in the capital, looking at every person, approaching homeless people, hoping against hope that they would find him.

When Dublin revealed no sign of Joseph, Michael took off to England. There had been a photo in a paper in England of someone who looked like Joseph and when Michael heard about it, he set out for London immediately. He spent the best part of a month combing the vast city. Like in Dublin, Michael travelled the streets, searching in all the places that homeless people were to be found, asking everyone he met if they had seen his son. After almost a month, Michael realised he could do no more there, he had looked everywhere and it was time to go back to Ireland. Michael registered Joseph with the missing services in the UK.

The search continued for years. Every reported sighting was investigated thoroughly and the family made enquiries everywhere but to no avail. They have no idea what happened to Joseph after he left the hospital in Castlebar that day.

People in the area were very upset by Joseph's disappearance. His family is well known, and there were countless offers of assistance. Joseph (or Joe-Joe as his father fondly calls him) used to be an active member of the local set dancing society, along with his father. The teachers, who travel the world teaching the dances, always made sure to bring plenty of posters of young Joseph with them, in the hope that someone might see the picture and know where he was.

Joseph's disappearance certainly did not appear planned. He had said nothing about going away to his parents. He hadn't taken a change of clothes or passport with him, nor did he have much money on him at the time of his disappearance.

Joseph was deeply loved by his family, all the more because he had been very sick since his mid-teens. One day, three years before his disappearance, Joseph had gone to school as usual. That afternoon, his parents received a call from the school to say Joseph was very ill and he had been taken to hospital. The teacher thought Joseph was about to have a heart attack. Instead, Joseph was diagnosed with the dreaded illness 'manic depression', now bi-polar disorder. Joseph was only 16 years old at the time.

His family were shocked at the gravity of the disease that had attacked their young son. The illness manifested itself very seriously in Joseph and he was sent for treatment to St. Anne's hospital in Galway. The hospital kept him as a patient for two years.

After that time, he was brought home to continue his treatment as a day patient in St. Teresa's in Castlebar. Life was difficult for the Kelly family as Joseph's mood could never be predicted and he had to be watched all of the time. The whole family loved Joseph dearly and did everything they could to help him.

His siblings, Martina now 40, Anna, 33, Padraig, 32, and Michael, 26, always got on very well with Joseph. Since being diagnosed with bi-polar disorder he had become a lot more difficult. They never knew what effect the illness would have on Joseph from one day to the next: 'He could be awkward at times. It could put him in a good or bad humour.' His father recalls how Joseph could be difficult. 'He was sick. Sometimes he'd be alright but other times he couldn't help it. The whole family was very helpful.' But the family understood that it was a very serious illness and Joseph could do nothing about it. They were anxious to improve Joseph's life in any way they could and surrounded him with love and support.

'Joe-Joe' was very close to his father and, before he became very ill, they were involved in a lot of things together. Michael recalls fondly

how Joseph would come to set dancing classes
enjoyed the classes immensely. 'He was a good
bother. He also played football.' Michael also rem
helped him on the dairy farm before he got sick.

Once Joseph became sick, he was a changed person. He cou work on the farm or take part in sports anymore. His days were spent in the hospital. If he wasn't too bad, he would take part in creative sessions and make things; other days he would just lie on a bed, unable to take part in anything. There were times when Joseph was in a very bad way and the hospital would keep him in overnight. When he was at home, the family had to keep an eye on him constantly. Naturally, there was always the hope that Joseph would recover from the terrible illness and return to his normal self. 'People do pull through, but you never know.' It was very difficult for the family to see the previously happy boy they knew withdraw from regular life. They were often at a loss as all they could do was offer constant help, support and love to him. They often wished that they could wave a magic wand and cure him, make him happy again.

After more than 10 years, there is not much more the family can do to search for Joseph, physically they have explored every avenue. Now they remain in constant contact with missing persons organisations both in Ireland and abroad, always with the glimmer of hope that one day Joseph will turn up.

The Kelly family do all in their power to maintain a normal life, desperate to continue, though always plagued by the emptiness and bewilderment of not knowing where their son is. The teenage son who disappeared would be an adult in his 30s now.

Michael finds a lot of solace in keeping in contact with the families of other missing people. He says the efforts of people such as Jo Jo Dullard's sister, Mary Phelan, to get the police to do more is very important. Joseph was present at the opening of the monument to missing people, erected at Kilkenny Castle. He had his hands cast to be included along with all the handprints of other relatives of missing people on the monument.

Michael says life is very difficult. He does all in his power to get on with life and is determined to continue. He knows sitting in will not bring Joseph back. 'What can you do? You have to keep going, you have to get out, otherwise you'd crack up.' Michael continues going to set dancing classes, which he loves. Joseph's mother, Christina, is under huge strain. Michael thinks it is often more difficult for Christina. 'People react in different ways. Christina is more private. She prays a lot.'

In common with many other families, the 'not knowing' makes it all the harder. At least if they knew what had happened to Joseph, the Kellys could find closure. Naturally, they would do anything to find their son alive but, facing reality, they know there is another possibility. 'There was a phone call recently when a body was found in Achill. While on one level it was a relief that it wasn't him, on another I would find it a relief to find his body now and give him a proper burial.'

'I don't know where Joseph is', Michael says in a defeated voice. He turns to his wife: 'Christina where do you think he is?' Christina pauses for a moment 'I think Joseph is up in heaven.' Michael sighs, 'It's hard to know'.

27

Philip Cairns

'He had just started secondary school.'

Born 1973.
Missing from Rathfarnham, Dublin since 23 October, 1986.

Philip Cairns was just 13 years old when he disappeared in October 1986. Since then, Philip's disappearance has baffled investigators and has also been the subject of many strange and varied theories. Was he the victim of a paedophile ring? Was he kidnapped and forced to join a cult? Could he have fallen into a river? Could he have wandered off of his own accord and fallen in with the wrong people? And, most importantly, do any of his former schoolfriends know what happened to their classmate?

Philip left behind his parents, Alice and Philip Senior, his four sisters, Mary, Sandra, Helen and Suzanne, and a younger brother, Eoin.

It was the end of the school week, a Friday, when Philip left Coláiste Éanna Secondary School at 12.45 pm and returned to his home on Ballyroan Road for lunch. He finished eating and did some homework before leaving the house at 1.30 pm to walk back to school, but he never arrived.

His mother, Alice, was at home with his grandmother and his sister Suzanne. Alice was getting ready to take his sister into the city to see a dentist. As he left the house to return to school, Philip called goodbye to his grandmother. He had just started secondary school six weeks earlier and was settling in well.

Part of the difficulty on the day he disappeared was that no one realised Philip was missing until school had finished. His teachers may have missed him from their afternoon classes, but they would have assumed he had stayed at home after lunch. His family, on the other hand, had seen him leave to go back to school and would have had no reason to think that he didn't arrive. They thought he was safely in afternoon classes.

When he didn't come home that evening, his parents were very concerned. Alice went around to his friend's house hoping he had gone there after school, as pals do, but there was no sign of Philip. His friends told Alice that her son hadn't been in school in the afternoon. The father of Philip's pal was a garda and he immediately raised the alarm at Rathfarnham station.

A search got underway very quickly. Gardaí called to the Cairns' house and a full alert went out, asking gardaí everywhere to look out for the boy.

One of the mysteries is how a teenage boy could just disappear on what is a very busy road. Philip's mother is convinced that somebody saw something, knows something that could put their hearts at rest, could tell them what happened to Philip, even after all these years. For that reason, his family has always been happy to talk to reporters, hoping that someone out there will have their memory jogged and will remember that they saw something that day, something which probably didn't seem suspicious at the time, maybe a teenager taking a lift or a boy walking right past his school. There is also always the feeling that some other pupil at the school may have seen something, but may not have wanted to speak out at the time in case they got Philip into trouble, maybe someone who thought he was going to mitch school for the afternoon.

A very extensive search operation was organised by the Gardaí and hundreds of local people and sub aqua divers were involved in searching rivers, lakes, forests and the Dublin Mountains. There were over 400 sightings reported and all of them were followed up. A neighbour of the Cairns family kindly persuaded the milk companies to distribute posters of Philip. There were also house-to-house searches in the area, but nothing came from all of this.

It was mid-term break at Coláiste Éanna but, on the Wednesday after Philip's disappearance, the pupils were asked to return voluntarily to school to meet with the Gardaí. The Gardaí wanted to talk to them about Philip's disappearance and to find out if any of them knew anything about it, but none of the pupils were able to assist.

A very strange thing happened that afternoon, however. Following the garda visit to the school, Philip's school bag appeared in a laneway off Anne Devlin Road, close to his home. It was found by two schoolgirls. But the perplexing thing is this – the laneway had already been searched and there had been no sign of any bag.

The bag contained some of Philip's books, but his geography book and two religion books were missing. There were forensic tests carried out on the bag but there were no new revelations. Even now the Gardaí are extremely anxious to know who placed Philip's bag in the laneway; they may not even understand the importance of the information they possess.

It is also possible that one of the students interviewed by gardaí that day had taken the bag but decided to return it after meeting with them. It is equally important that they come forward now, as an adult, to tell Gardaí where the bag was found originally. Even the original location of the bag could help in solving the mystery of their former classmate's abduction. Of course, these school pals are now young men, some have their own families and it must cross their minds occasionally that the Cairns family is still suffering the loss of their child. Even today the Gardaí stress that any information could be important.

On each anniversary of Philip's disappearance, there are extensive appeals for information and, in 1999, his case was the subject of an episode of the RTÉ programme *Solved and Unsolved*.

Philip has missed many family occasions. His parents now have two grandchildren he has never met, and the effect over the years on his sisters and brother is described by his mother as 'very tough'. All through the years of growing up, doing exams, making new friends, this has been hanging over them and it's still there.

The family has suffered through false hopes and hoax calls, incredibly cruel but nevertheless a fact of life for some families of missing people. There have been suggestions that Philip was abducted by a paedophile ring that was operating in the area at the time of his disappearance, but there has never been any proof of this put forward. There have been articles written about Satanism and other cults, none of them substantiated, but all causing further heartache to the family.

Today, if Philip is still alive, he is in his 30s and no doubt looks very different. Experts have been able to 'age' Philip to show some idea of what he might look like now. These 'photos' have been widely publicised in the hope that, even as an adult, someone might recognise Philip.

If he is alive, if he is living someplace else, what thoughts go through his mind? Does he remember what happened? Has he any way of making contact with home?

For his parents, the heartbreak goes on and yet somebody somewhere may be able to end it and refuses to do so. But his mother hasn't given up hope of finding Philip alive, 'I still hope', she says. 'He wouldn't have gone away on his own.'

A computer-generated image of what Philip Cairns might look like as an adult

28

Bettina Poeschel

'Fate can meet anybody anywhere – even on a sunny afternoon.'

Missing from Newgrange from 25 September to 16 October, 2001. Found deceased.

Just over two years ago a young German journalist, Bettina Poeschel, went missing while visiting Ireland. There was an extensive search which, sadly, ended with the discovery of the 28-year-old's body in dense undergrowth near Newgrange in Co. Meath.

The search for Bettina lasted just three weeks but, even in that space of time, her family went through the hell of not knowing what had happened to her and local people had to face the horrifying realisation that a young tourist may have been murdered in their locality.

Bettina went missing on 25 September, 2001, after she left Dublin to travel to Newgrange via Drogheda. The last confirmed sighting was as she walked along the main Dublin–Belfast road close to Drogheda bus station where, it is believed, she intended either to catch a shuttle bus to the Brú na Bóinne visitor centre near Newgrange, or else walk the 10-kilometre route the bus takes to the centre. There are no CCTV cameras in the visitor centre to establish whether or not she actually reached it.

A week later Gardaí appealed to tourists who visited the visitor centre to check their videos and photographs for images of the German woman. Around 500 people passed through the centre on the day she disappeared and Gardaí were hoping that someone who took pictures or videos there might have accidentally included Bettina. 'We are appealing to people to either look at their pictures or videos for anyone fitting Bettina's description or to give them to us', said Garda Superintendent Fergus Doggitt at the time.

Gardaí also set up a series of checkpoints at Brú na Bóinne and Donore village in the hope of jogging the memory of someone who perhaps only travelled through the area on a weekly basis.

Bettina's family travelled to Ireland to assist in the search, desperately hoping she was still alive. Her father Jurgen and sister Cornelia said it was totally out of character for her not to have made contact with her family and friends. Four days after his daughter disappeared, Jurgen said they were afraid of the worst. Cornelia said that although Bettina would not normally accept a lift from someone, she may have on this occasion because of the 10-kilometre distance from the visitor centre to Drogheda.

Before leaving for Ireland, Bettina had spent three days with her family in Munich. On the Sunday she disappeared, her sister received a text message from her, and that was to be her last contact with her family.

It was in the early hours of the Wednesday morning, a few hours after Bettina failed to return to her friend Holger Sirth's flat in Dublin where she was staying, that the alarm was raised. Holger checked her room but there was no sign that she had been there. He immediately contacted her family in Munich and the Gardaí.

Bettina was to leave Dublin on the Wednesday morning, flying out at 7.30 am. Her ticket was still with her luggage in the flat. She had not contacted the airline to cancel and her mobile phone was not being answered.

Bettina loved her work as a journalist. She was a very creative person and had a great interest in the arts, in politics and in travelling. She came to Ireland to visit places of historical interest and had already visited Glendalough and the James Joyce trail in Dublin.

As soon as she was reported missing to the Gardaí, a massive search got underway. The Garda dog unit, the air support unit and the sub aqua unit between them combed the roads, the fields and the river from Newgrange to Drogheda. Questionnaires were handed out and there were house-to-house enquiries. Locals were asked to check sheds and outbuildings on their properties.

Gardaí said there was nothing to link Bettina's disappearance to that of the other young women who have vanished without trace in recent years.

However, there was tragedy in store for Bettina's family just three weeks later when Gardaí discovered the battered body of a young woman in woodland near Donore, just 40 yards from the roadway.

The body was partially decomposed and had been disturbed by animals. Various theories were considered at the time including the possibility that she could have been the victim of a hit and run driver who had then hidden her body.

DNA testing and dental records identified the body to be that of Bettina. Her father had given a blood sample on a previous visit to Ireland and this helped in a positive identification. A man has now been charged with her murder and that trial is expected to take place in early 2004.

The people of this quiet corner of Co. Meath were shocked and felt a deep sense of loss at the killing of a young tourist in their midst. Some months after her death, Bettina's father sent an open letter to the people of Donore. He invited Irish artists to help create a monument to his daughter.

'We hope that we can erect a dignified memorial near the place she has been found, hopefully based on the ideas of young local artists. We want them to show how fate can meet anybody anywhere, for instance on a sunny afternoon on a frequented road among hospitable Irish people.'

For Bettina's second anniversary, her memorial stone was erected in a small grotto-like place on the Drogheda to Donore road, the road Bettina would have walked to visit Newgrange.

There were flowers on the branches and trunks of trees that overhung the headstone and on that stone were more flowers and a wreath from her family. It had a small silk scarf attached.

And there was a card:

Bettina – the sweetest flower in God's garden.

The memorial stone itself is five feet high and has a small picture of Bettina embedded in it. It says Bettina 'was killed here on a sunny afternoon on 25th September 2001.'

Then there is a quotation from James Joyce.

The Why of the World
Is an answerless riddle
Puzzlesome,
Tiresome,
Hard to unriddle.

29

Thomas Linehan

'It meant we were able to give him a Christian burial.'

Missing from Cork from 3 January to 14 April, 2001.
Found deceased.

David Linehan, the middle child among three sisters, Carmel, Marie and Sinéad, and a brother, Dara, was just a teenager when he became involved in search and rescue operations on the River Lee in Cork city. Little did he think then that it would fall to him some years later to pull his own father's body from the river.

David says you never think something like this will happen in your own family. He recalls listening to a man on the radio making an appeal for information on his missing brother. 'I was getting my hair cut and I heard a local man, Cormac Cremin, talk about his missing brother, Pearse, on the radio. Pearse was a well-known tennis coach in Cork City. I sympathised with him, but I could never have imagined that our family would be in a similar situation in a matter of months.'

David's father, Thomas, worked with Cork Harbour Commission as berthing master. He was used to working on the water and, because of the nature of his work, had sometimes recovered bodies from the harbour. On 3 January, 2001, 61-year-old Thomas went missing. His wife, Philomena, raised the alarm and a number of searches got underway. David knew how to search and immediately brought out all the sub aqua groups, the Gardaí and many friends and colleagues, but nothing was found.

Ironically, Cormac Cremin, whose interview David had listened to on the radio, became one of David's strongest supporters, taking over the task of putting up search posters for Thomas on one side of the city as well as assisting in the search.

More than three months later, on 14 April, a local man was out picking periwinkles when he discovered a man's foot at the edge of the water. This type of discovery is pretty horrific, but at the same time the family of a missing person welcomes it as it may lead to the location of their loved one's body, which is what happened in this case.

The search for Thomas was then concentrated on the area where the foot had been discovered, with David and the rest of the sub aqua team going through the area meticulously, looking for any clues in the water. Four days later, David found the rest of his father's remains and was able to retrieve them and bring them ashore.

David believes it was a good thing that it was he who found his father as he had done this type of work before and also because he felt privileged in being able to render this last service to his father.

'It had to be done', he says, 'and I was used to that kind of work. It was closure for the family. Finding my father deceased was a relief and meant we were able to give him a Christian burial.'

Although David says the loss of his father 'destroyed the whole family', he says 'the worst part of it when he was missing, the greatest pain of all, was not knowing what had happened or where he was. We were heartbroken when his remains were found but we were glad to find out something. So many people go for years without knowing what has happened to a loved one.'

When his own father disappeared, David felt keenly the lack of resources available to assist in the search for a missing person and the delay in getting a search underway. But 'rather than whinge about it' as he puts it himself, 'I felt it was up to us to do something to make things better, to have better communications with all those involved.'

David immediately set about making contact with the various arms of the rescue services, the dogs unit and the divers, bringing them all together.

Today the rescue services in the Cork area are well co-ordinated and ready to go into search mode at a moment's notice and will travel all over the country if necessary. Sadly they have recovered six bodies from the River Lee over the last two years. At the end of last year, they assisted local services in searching the River Slaney in Enniscorthy, Co. Wexford where five people went missing in separate incidents, recovering two of them.

On a personal basis, the Linehan family had already been through hell. Thomas' niece (and David's cousin) Michelle McCormick, went missing in July 1993.

Michelle's body has never been recovered and, although a man was charged with her murder, the subsequent trial collapsed. Michelle left behind a little girl who is now 11 years old.

'You never get over it', David says, 'you have to learn how to live with it. My family went through it twice.'

With the assistance of Cormac Cremin, David recently set up a support network for families of missing persons to provide comfort and advice to people who are going through a harrowing experience. Group members can call each other, day or night, to discuss their feelings of confusion, loss and anxiety.

David says he couldn't have made it through the pain of his own loss without the assistance of both Cormac and Fr Aquinas Duffy. 'My conscience made me set up this support network in Cork', he says. 'Adequate counselling services just aren't there for people. Do you put your grief and confusion on hold? Families are suffering without being assisted by the state.'

Members of the support network are calling on the Minister for Justice to set up special regional missing persons units to deal exclusively with missing persons cases. This, the group members argue, would take the pressure off Gardaí by spreading the workload. An appeal has also been made to the Government to set up a special 24-hour helpline whereby a missing person can call and pass on information to their family.

30
Derek Browne

'We will all meet some day in heaven.'

Missing from Mullingar, Co. Westmeath from 6 June to 31 August, 2003. Found deceased.

This is one of the most recent cases of a young man who disappeared and it is also one of the most poignant. I had interviewed Derek's father, Dermot, for this book while he was still hopeful that his son would be found. However, just a couple of weeks later, Derek's body was found in his home town of Mullingar. Nevertheless, I have included the full interview as it explains the various stages of the search for Derek. Ar dheis Dé go raibh a anam dílis.

At 7.30 am on 6 June, 2003, 27-year-old Derek Browne set out as usual to walk to work at Mullingar Pewter in Co. Westmeath. At half past three that afternoon his mother, Ann, went to his workplace to collect him and was told that he hadn't been in work.

She went home and found that Derek had left two notes in which he said that he couldn't stand the pain of separation from his girlfriend (they had recently broken up). He went on to say that he was sorry for what he was about to do, but they would all meet some day in heaven. Friends later told the family that Derek had said he intended to throw himself into the canal.

The canal is where the search then began. The Garda helicopter was called out and the family, now in a state of panic, drove around the local lakes. At 5 am the next morning, Derek's brother Dermot Junior, his dad and his uncle walked the canal. It was cold, breezy and miserable as they trekked the 13 miles, but they found nothing.

That night the family's spirit rose a little after a reported sighting of Derek in the town. Moving away from the idea that Derek had taken his own life the family now wondered if an incident a few days earlier could have had something to do with his disappearance. Derek had been assaulted and kicked in the head leaving him with a swollen face and head and a black eye. His brother saw his injuries when he went into his bedroom but Derek didn't want to do anything about it. He did, however, tell his brother that he knew who had assaulted him.

That was the end of that, although the family later wondered if he had been suffering from concussion because of the blow to his head.

The family printed and distributed posters, did interviews with the media and kept searching. Dermot lashed out at the lack of resources available to help families like the Brownes, 'In Ireland you're left to your own devices. It is abysmal, you need that help in the first few hours when you don't know what to be doing.'

During this time the family went through hell. 'I kept asking is he out in the rain? Is he cold? Is he alright? Is he dead? I spent days alone in the woods following the advice of clairvoyants. I went over the area in a light plane, Dermot Jnr set up a chain e-mail system with a poster of Derek scanned in.'

Dermot pinned his hopes on the attack on his son, hoping that if the bang on the head had caused a lapse of memory, then Derek might be living rough in Dublin. So he traipsed around the city, searching among the homeless and the hostels. One day he spent eight hours just walking around the city looking into the face of every homeless person he met, hoping he would see Derek's eyes looking back at him. He also wondered what Derek could look like. Would he have grown his hair? A beard? Would he recognise him? There were no leads in Dublin but Dermot planned to go back and carry out a more organised search of the places where homeless people congregate.

In the meantime, a group of prison officers from Dublin's Mountjoy prison kindly offered to meet in Dublin to comb the city for Derek.

Another local search got underway on Saturday, 30 August. There were many different areas to examine but Dermot says they were continually drawn back to the canal. Nothing was found and the family came home happy. 'At least he's alive', Dermot said. 'Now it's just a question of finding him.'

But that hope was shattered with a phone call from a local woman who said she had found a pair of shoes beside Lough Ennel. She knew about Derek's disappearance and asked Dermot to have a look at them. He did and, no, they weren't Derek's. As he travelled home, a fire brigade passed in the opposite direction.

The Brownes had become addicted to teletext, checking all the time to see if a body had been found anywhere in the country. So when they arrived home, Dermot turned on the TV and was horrified to learn that a body had been recovered from the sea at Greystones in Co. Wicklow. 'You wonder "Is that my lad?"' he says.

But before he could even investigate the identity of the body washed up in Greystones, there was a knock at the door. Two local gardaí had arrived with the bad news, Derek's body had been found. It was hanging in a tree beside the canal at Baltrasna, about three miles from Mullingar. He had been found by a young girl and her parents who were walking their dog in the area and got a strong smell from nearby. They weren't sure what it was, they had noticed it on a previous occasion as well and the girl ran towards the trees to follow the smell. She found Derek hanging from a tree.

Derek's body had been concealed in a flat area. A bush grew in front of the tree where he was hanging. 'There was a peculiar kind of feeling – relief and then a feeling of hopelessness', says Dermot.

Dermot doesn't know whether Derek committed suicide or not. There was a strange phone call that day from a man with a Dublin accent who asked questions about who had beaten Derek up at the beginning of June. This anonymous caller said that Derek had been abducted and murdered and could be found two miles outside Mullingar. He was close in relation to the distance. But who was he? Did he know something about the attack on Derek? Was he involved in the attack? Or could it be even more sinister, did he know something about Derek's death? Had Derek really committed suicide or was there somebody else involved in his death?

The family visited clairvoyants. One of them said the body would be found just half a mile from where it was eventually found. Dermot had also visited a healing priest who told him that Derek was in heaven and 'closer to you now than he ever was'. He told the devastated father that some good was going to come out of it.

The young man was buried alongside his grandfather. Although he hadn't been noticeably close to him in life, Derek had kept his grandfather's framed memoriam card beside his bed and had visited the grave just days before he went missing.

At the graveside, the family spoke to their son, telling him they loved him and knew he was in heaven, but begging for some sign that he was at peace. Later that night the diviner who had been closest to where the body was found, rang to say that he had sensed that Derek was dead but didn't want to upset the family at the time by telling them. 'The reason I'm ringing now', he said, 'is to tell you that Derek is in heaven and at peace.' They had their sign.

The following day Dermot went back to the grave. He said to Derek, 'Son, I love you. I don't know why you did it. I'm sorry you didn't ask for help. My heart is broken.'

He was still unaware, however, of the full horror of the manner of Derek's death. He decided to visit the spot where Derek had been found and he saw something on the ground with a cloud of flies buzzing around it.

On closer inspection he was devastated to discover his son's body fluids and fragments of his brain lying around the tree and covered in flies. Dermot had worked in the ambulance service at one stage, so he knew what he was looking at. He was also very upset when he saw the blue latex gloves used by the rescue workers just thrown into the ditch. 'Do these people ever think there is a family going to go out there and see all this?' he asks. He shovelled up his son's remains, dug a hole and buried them. He then covered them with stones and planted flowers on the spot.

Now Dermot is determined that Derek won't have died in vain. He says the efforts of all the rescue services need to be co-ordinated and the links recognised between the missing, the homeless and the suicidal.

'We need a central organisation formed from people who know what it's like to have a loved one missing. Straight away, someone should go out to them, empathise with them and liaise with them in a more humane manner. There should be connections with all the rescue services including the sub aqua clubs and dog handlers. There should be photos published immediately instead of a description of height and colouring – sure that's no use if you're hoping someone will spot them walking down the street. And the initial search needs to be intense. If a proper search had been done, my son would have been found sooner.'

However, Dermot is fulsome in his praise for the people who helped search for his son. 'People in Mullingar are great, even the elderly turned up and offered to help and people travelled miles to collect posters and put them up.'

Dermot also has this gentle advice for parents: 'Learn the signs and symptoms of depression and if you see the slightest sign of it, get help. Men don't seem to cry for help.'

Dermot and Ann now keep a lighted candle in Derek's bedroom window, they say it will be lit 'as long as we live'.

The spot where Derek died has now become something of a shrine. People have left messages for him there and others just drop by to say a prayer for him.

Dermot has also addressed Mullingar Town Council to push for better education in schools and more interaction from the Health Boards in order to educate young people about suicide and depression and to know what signs to look out for in their friends.

'When Derek told his friends about what he was going to do, it was obviously a cry for help', he says, 'but they didn't know what to do.'

Dermot also wants to ask television stations to devote just 30 seconds a week to showing two or three pictures of people who are missing. He stresses again and again that a description of the person without their photo is useless in terms of getting swift recognition of someone who has gone missing.

Derek's younger brother, 26-year-old Dermot Jnr has written the following piece and posted it on the Missing Persons website.

I miss Derek terribly, as do all of my family. In Derek's final days he must have been tormented by what he was about to do. He loved God, his family and the friends he had around him. He was a kind and friendly guy who had time for everybody.

I spent months crying myself to sleep. Trying to hide my feelings from my family who were hurting. That pain of a missing brother has now been replaced by the pain of a lost brother. The fact that I will never to able to see or speak to my brother again tears me apart every day.

I wish he had reached out to me or anyone and told us what he was going through. There are so many questions, questions I know there are no answers to, but I must ask all the same.

I pray that all the families of missing persons do not have to go through what we went through and continue to go through. If you are a missing person, please call somebody. A family member or a close one, just to let your family know you are alive. It really would make their pain more bearable.

If you are the family of a missing person or a recently lost relative, my heart truly goes out to you. Indeed I offer my prayers and kind thoughts to you all each night and I hope and wish you well. I ask you all to pause after reading this and pray to your God for the safe return of these missing persons and spare a kind thought for my dear brother Derek.

Derek, I miss you always and love you very much. Forever in my heart.

Your loving younger brother, Dermot.

31

Tim O'Connell

'Mam, I have a girl.'

Missing from Ballyphehane, Co. Cork from 17 December, 2002 to April 2003. Found deceased.

On 17 December, 2002, the whole country was getting ready to celebrate Christmas. That was the day that 42-year-old Tim O'Connell vanished and the last time mother of four, Monica Flynn, from Ballyphehane in Cork city saw her partner of nearly 20 years.

The couple had been making the usual preparations for Christmas and Monica didn't notice anything unusual. They had a cup of tea and a sandwich before they went to bed that night. Then, at 2.30 am, Tim got out of bed and left the house in a wine-coloured Toyota Carina. It wasn't that strange, Tim was a taxi driver and worked irregular hours, he also often popped out for a packet of cigarettes. So, initially,

Monica didn't think anything was wrong. But the alarm was raised later that morning when Tim failed to return to the family home.

Christmas came but Monica said it was a time of great sorrow and confusion as she and her children, Shane (13), Edward (12) and Niamh (3) waited in vain for news on Tim's whereabouts.

Monica had had a very hard year. Her eldest son, Trevor, had lost his battle with muscular dystrophy the previous year at only 18 years of age. She missed Tim all the more. She says he was a marvellous stepfather to Trevor, caring for him right through his illness.

Monica said at the time that in spite of the heartache of losing their son, she couldn't imagine why Tim would go missing, that before his disappearance Tim seemed perfectly normal and was looking forward to Christmas. She said she was trying to keep to a routine, to keep things going and that it was little Niamh who was keeping her spirits up but it was 'very tough'. She said the little girl still called for her father, three months after he disappeared.

Tim came from a close family and regularly went for a drink and a game of cards with his four brothers in a pub in Ballyphehane. His mother, Kitty, was totally baffled by her son's disappearance as he was a real family man who loved Monica and the kids. 'When Tim's little girl was born he was thrilled', she says, 'He came home and said "Mam, I have a girl". He couldn't believe it, he was delighted, he loves his children.'

Kitty was unfortunate enough to receive a number of hoax telephone calls a few days after Tim vanished and was convinced her son was on the end of the line.

Pictures of Tim were placed in the windows of taxicabs around Cork City and his friends and colleagues assisted in the search. His bank account remained untouched and he didn't take luggage or his passport with him. The day before he disappeared, he handed over €3,500 in car insurance.

Tim's sister, Tracey, was also baffled by her brother's disappearance and she added her voice to the rest of the family in an appeal to Tim to come home. 'It is not just a brother going missing', she said at the time, 'it is very hard to look at my 72-year-old mum. After all, Tim is still her child at the end of the day. If he needs time out we would understand that.'

Sadly, the search for Tim ended in tragedy when his body was taken from the River Lee at Easter time. His sister Tracey, along with the rest of the family, has done a great deal of fundraising work, raising thousands of euro for the Cork Missing Persons Association. Despite the loss of Tim, the fundraising will go towards helping other families to find their loved ones who have disappeared.

32

Nora Mary King

'Any chance of a cup of tea?

Missing from Monagea, Newcastlewest,
Co. Limerick from 14–17 August, 2003.
Found unharmed.

'Any chance of a cup of tea?' were the first words of Nora Mary King when she knocked on the door of a farmhouse after spending three nights and four days sleeping in the fields and living on wild berries. This is one of those stories with a happy ending, but it is also one that gripped the hearts of everyone who heard that the 80-year-old grandmother had gone missing in the remote but beautiful countryside close to her home at Monagea, Newcastlewest, Co. Limerick.

The search began in high spirits but, four days later, many of the searchers had begun to fear the worst and, alongside the feeling that

Nora had just gone for a walk or to visit neighbours, the possibility of something sinister began to creep into everyone's mind. Abduction and murder were two such possibilities that struck the searchers as they walked about calling her name during those long dark warm nights. There was no tangible reason for them to think like that, of course, but they had all heard tales of pensioners being attacked and killed for just a few pence.

It was mid-August, high summer and the country was enjoying glorious warm weather when Nora Mary King went missing from the home she shared with her son, Pat. The widowed mother of seven children had been suffering some slight memory loss of late, but there had been no cause for alarm. She was in great health otherwise, agile and independent.

A number of family members live in the immediate area. She has four sons, Brian, Bill, John and Pat, and three daughters, Kate, Betty and Maureen, as well as 16 grandchildren.

On Thursday, 14 August, Nora got up as usual and went to Mass, something she has done almost every day of her life.

Her son John and his wife, Mary, were at a wedding that day in Killarney and during the evening they got a phone call from John's brother, Pat, to say that Nora was missing. The following day was the Feast of the Assumption and Nora would normally have gone to the vigil Mass the evening before. But she hadn't turned up at Mass and, it transpired, hadn't been seen since 9.30 that morning.

The fact that some members of the family were at the wedding meant there were less people around than usual to see her coming and going.

Pat had had a good look around but couldn't find any sign of his mother. She is a very fit woman, cycles her bike everywhere and walks every day, not the typical image of an 80-year-old woman at all.

John and Mary left the wedding in Killarney and drove the 35 miles home to Monagea. Mary says they weren't worried at that stage. 'We didn't panic or anything. We thought she would be found by the time we came home and that she'd be there waiting for us.'

They arrived home shortly afterwards, but there was still no sign of Nora. In the meantime, her bike had been found in a ditch a short distance away.

The Gardaí were alerted and a huge search got underway in the hilly countryside and particularly around the area where Nora grew up in the old family home, which is near a steep hill at Rathcahill, only two miles from where Nora lives now. The old house is long deserted, but there is a relative living nearby in a new house.

The family now believes that Nora was heading for her relative's house. She knew that her brother was home on holiday from England and was staying with that relative so she had probably decided to visit him. 'We think she was going to that house and she knew where she was going, but she probably forgot about it on the way up', says Mary.

The family was aware that Nora was suffering from memory loss, a mild form of senile dementia, but stress that she is a very independent woman who is able to do everything for herself without assistance.

Family, friends and neighbours searched right through the night but couldn't find any sign of Nora. At six o'clock the next morning they were joined by the helicopter from Valentia Coast Guard.

'We still believed she would be found alive', says Mary, 'we knew she was a resilient woman.'

The good weather of those few days is probably what kept Nora alive, but it could also be the reason she became disoriented when she tried to visit her relative close to the old family homestead. Nobody knows how she stayed alive but she probably survived on wild berries and drank water from local streams. 'She is a woman who would be well able to look after herself, a very resourceful person', says Mary, 'so although we were worried, we kept that in the front of our minds as well.'

The search, co-ordinated by Inspector Ann Marie McMahon, went on all day Friday. The mountain rescue teams, the civil defence, the sniffer dogs from the Search and Rescue Dog Association and the Garda dog unit all arrived. The searchers were then asked to leave the area because there would be too many different scents to distract the dogs.

It was Friday, 15 August, the local Pattern day when, traditionally, people visit the blessed well in the area. Hundreds of people turned up to pray at the well for Nora's safe return. There was no sign of her by nightfall and it was the second night out in the open for Nora, certainly worry was beginning to seep in at this stage.

On Saturday morning the family say the search became more organised, up to one thousand people turned out to help. The Garda helicopter was carrying out a search from the air and volunteers were divided up so that each segment of the locality was searched thoroughly.

'At that stage it was getting serious', Mary said 'but the Civil Defence kept our spirits up. They kept reassuring us that Nora had great survival instincts, they gave us hope.' Then a 12-year-old local boy, Dermot Considine, found Nora's glasses when he was out searching with his father.

The family contacted their brother, Bill, who lives in the Philippines and he decided to travel home. He arrived in Limerick at two o'clock on Sunday afternoon having had a 24-hour flight to think the worst. Nora had now been missing for four days and three nights. All the churches in the area had made appeals for information about her and flyers with her photograph had been distributed.

Then the miracle happened. At five o'clock that afternoon, Sunday, 17 August, Nora knocked on the front door of a house five miles from her home and asked, 'Would there be any chance of a cup of tea?' John Joe and Maura Sexton had been watching a match on television when Nora arrived. They had been out earlier helping to search for her.

John Joe asked her who she was and realised immediately that it was Nora, the missing woman. They brought her in and she drank four cups of tea while the Sextons passed on the good news to gardaí. Nora was very tired and very thirsty and her clothes had bits of twigs and vegetation caught on them where she had probably slept out in the fields overnight.

But Nora didn't realise she was missing. She kept asking what all the fuss was about. She thought she had only been gone for a few hours, that was her concept of time. She was very sunburnt and her lips were burned as a result of having been out in the open for four days.

'It was the heat that caught her and really confused her', says Mary. 'The sun and the bit of forgetfulness combined. She thought she had visited a cousin of the family, an older relation, and she thought that's where she had been.' And that would have been typical of Nora's caring attitude, 'She looked after loads of people in her day, her mother and her mother-in-law, as well as her own husband who died 12 years ago when he was only 71.'

The search centre was the local community centre. Mary and John had just returned there from a stint of searching when the good news arrived. 'One of the mountain rescue lads got up on a wall and said they might have good news, that they had a sighting of Nora but it still had to be confirmed, and when it was, a great cheer went up', says Mary.

People from a huge area, from neighbouring parishes up to 20 miles away had joined in the search, and the business people of the surrounding towns had been extraordinarily generous, providing food and drink for the searchers. They sent out cooked chickens, filled rolls, a fruit and vegetable company sent apples and bananas and Ballygowan sent bottled water.

Local farmers opened their fields as car parks as coach loads of volunteers joined the search. And the searchers were thrilled at the happy outcome; they were so relieved that the sprightly grandmother had been found safe and well that there were quite a few tears around Monagea. One young lad asked the family: 'Do you know when we'd do something wrong, Nora would give you a big hug and then she'd start giving out – did you think of doing that?'

Nora was taken to the doctor for a check up. He said she was in perfect health and told her to go home and rest and take plenty of fluids. The family say she was very tired for about a week afterwards.

Now Nora has resumed her normal life, knitting, cooking and going to Mass every morning. The only difference is that a member of the family is there all the time just to keep an eye on things.

Nora is still embarrassed though when people come up to her in the shops and ask 'aren't you the woman who was missing?', she tells them 'I was *not* missing!'

Mary Nora King with her bicycle

33

The Story of Tom

The Missing Husband

Michelle's husband, Tom, walked out on her 12 years ago. They had been married for 15 years and had two children, aged 14 and 10. Michelle says the marriage 'wasn't great' but wasn't too bad either. 'It was something similar to many of our friends, the mad love thing had gone off the boil and we were settled, fairly comfortable with one another and all our time was taken up with the mortgage and the kids.'

It was just after Christmas when Tom disappeared. 'He had been quiet over Christmas; I thought there was something wrong, I kept walking in when he was on the phone and he would immediately hang up saying "thanks, I'll pass that message on" and things like that. When I questioned him he said it was someone from work who needed to change their shifts, that kind of thing.'

On 30 December, Tom said he was going to the office for something and that was the last Michelle and the children heard of him. Tom travelled a lot so Michelle wasn't overly worried about his trip into work. 'He wasn't a great communicator at the best of times and that didn't concern me too much, he was involved in getting shipments and container loads in and out at strange hours sometimes, so that was okay.' But the next day there was still no sign of Tom and Michelle started to ring around. His mother told her he had called in the previous day 'on his way to work' but there was no further news.

When she checked his wardrobe, Michelle found quite a few clothes missing but again this wasn't so strange, 'he often carried a case of clothes around with him when he was travelling'. But what did concern her was a little photo she kept beside her bed, it showed herself and Tom and the kids, 'when that was gone, I realised something was seriously wrong; Tom wouldn't have taken that unless he wasn't coming back'.

A close friend asked Michelle bluntly if she thought there was somebody else, 'Don't be daft' was her answer.

A week later when everyone was back at work, Michelle spoke to his colleagues. They expressed surprise at her enquiries. Tom had handed in his notice before Christmas and told them he had a new job starting in January but didn't say where.

Michelle never reported Tom as a missing person and now she wonders why. 'I never actually called the Gardaí, I never thought anything bad had happened to him, somewhere inside I just knew he had gone away of his own accord', she says.

Tom's brother was a tower of strength, checking all over the UK with similar firms to see if there was any sign of him.

Their joint bank account hadn't been touched but an enormous surprise came at the end of January when somebody paid the mortgage. The bank didn't think anything of it, it was just another lodgement. Apparently, it had just been a cash payment and they were unable to trace any account as a result.

Michelle realised that Tom was obviously out there somewhere but not making contact. Then money started to appear in their joint account.

'I have to say this – despite the fact that I was in bits with the worry of it all, Tom never left us short. I didn't have to worry about money, it wasn't an issue. But the kids missed him, they kept asking questions and I didn't know what to tell them. They were too big to be fobbed off with "daddy's gone to work" type answers.

'Finally, I told them the truth, that he had gone away and I didn't know why. Tom's family were marvellous, they made sure the kids were well taken care of, they dropped in and chatted, they were there for me whenever I needed them. But I still agonised over where he was and my friend's question at the beginning when she asked me if Tom had met somebody else just haunted me.'

It was the following October before Michelle found out the truth.

One Tuesday afternoon she was just cleaning up the house before the kids came in from school. 'I will never forget it, I had defrosted the fridge the night before and there were newspapers all over the kitchen floor. The phone rang and I answered it, it was Tom! I didn't know what to say but somehow, at times like that, nature takes over and I just sobbed and sobbed at the sound of his voice.'

Tom told her then that he still cared about her, cared about the kids and wanted to see them but that he wasn't coming home. However, he didn't tell her everything. A few days later Tom contacted his brother and made arrangements to meet him in Dublin.

He told his brother that he had met someone else on his frequent travels around the UK. He had been very anxious that last Christmas because his girlfriend was pregnant and about to give birth to a baby daughter. As soon as the child was born he had travelled over to the UK to be with her.

Tom said he regretted what had happened, he was going to divorce Michelle but he wanted to see the kids sometimes. He said he would never leave Michelle stuck and would always be there for her but his life was with his new girlfriend and their baby daughter now.

There were no meetings with Michelle and she refused to have anything to do with him, but she eventually decided that it was in her own children's best interest to have contact with their father. For the next few years she allowed them to travel to the UK for holidays, 'but the worst bit was when they'd come back with stories about their new sister. They brought photos too and I must admit I had a sneaky look at them when the kids were in bed.'

Now, 12 years on, Tom and Michelle are divorced, the kids are grown up and Michelle has fallen in love again. However, she will never forget the months of heartache she went through wondering where Tom had gone and why. She says she was lucky in that if there were sides to be taken, Tom's family sided with her and gave her their total support.

There are still some obstacles to get round however. She doesn't know what will happen if their children decide to marry. 'Will he bring her? And their daughter? Maybe we'll both bring our new partners. Hopefully it's a long way into the future and we'll have time to get used to the idea.'

Michelle says it's not as raw now as it used to be, 'we've moved on', she says, 'but it was still a terrible thing to happen, it was the worst year of my life'.

34

The Story of Anne

Found by her children after 23 years

In December 2002, 56-year-old Anne O'Toole received a letter in the post. Nothing unusual in that, but she froze when she realised that it was addressed to her in her married name from her first marriage, a name she hadn't used in over 20 years.

It had been a tough marriage. Anne grew up in Northern Ireland, near Belfast. She met and married young and had four children before the situation between herself and her husband got totally out of control. 'Their daddy and I never got on', she says. 'Our marriage was finished and the only way I could get away from him was to go over to England.'

Anne had no money and couldn't find a way to bring her children with her. Her husband was physically abusive and Anne often had to hide out in women's refuge shelters until his temper subsided. She wants to forget the details but says it was 'a rough time'. When she left home in 1979, her children were aged 14, 13, 12 and 11.

With the help of some friends, Anne got to London and found a job as a domestic in a hospital there. She tried to keep in touch with her children and in 1980 she travelled over to Northern Ireland to see them and to tell them she had met someone else and was about to re-marry. When her ex-husband heard she was back, 'he kicked me out and the children had to hold him while I got out of the house'.

In 1980, Anne and her new husband, Dan, married and went to live in Africa. It was a different world and an exciting one. Dan offered to take on the entire family, all of Anne's children, none of whom he had ever met. For the children that would mean leaving Northern Ireland and at that stage the children were too settled in their lives, reluctant to change schools or to leave family and friends behind.

So Anne and Dan went to start their new life in Africa alone. Dan had a good job and was also continuing with his studies. Anne was absolutely delighted to discover she was pregnant. She gave birth to Rachel, her fifth child but Dan's first, and he absolutely idolised his beautiful baby daughter. But although they were very happy, Anne had a constant heartache, the loss of her first family.

Anne managed to stay in touch with her eldest daughter, Paula, for a time, but then it became very difficult. Her daughters all married, changing their names in the process, and to make matters worse, her son moved away from home. Letters were sent but they were never passed on to her children and they all lost contact with one another. Her first husband was still living in the family home.

'It was very hard losing contact', says Anne, 'but you always hope you'll make contact with them again and I always knew one day we'd be reunited. I used to write to my eldest daughter, Paula, and she could keep me informed of the other children but when we returned from Africa and I tried writing to Paula, my letters were returned saying that she didn't live there anymore. Obviously I thought that she had moved but I never gave up hope.'

So back to that letter. When Anne saw her former married name she knew it was something to do with her previous life. 'I opened it up and it was from the Salvation Army. The children were trying to trace me because their daddy had died and they wanted to get in touch again.'

By now Anne and Dan's daughter, Rachel, was 22 and had had a baby boy of her own, Aaron. On the day the letter arrived, Rachel was staying with her mum and was there to try and buffer the sheer shock Anne felt. 'Luckily', she says, 'Rachel was off work that day. I was in a state. I couldn't talk. Rachel phoned the Salvation Army and they said to wait for a while before making contact with the other children. But Rachel couldn't wait any longer, she phoned Paula and spoke to her and I spoke to her and that started it all off.'

Rachel knew the truth about her mother and had always wanted to meet her brother and sisters. She knew they had all lost contact but was confident that they would get together at some stage. However, even she was not prepared for a letter arriving out of the blue. 'It was unbelievable', Anne says, 'I don't think I'll ever be able to describe how I felt then. It had been more than 20 years since I had spoken to any of my children.'

The extraordinary thing was that Anne discovered that not only did she have grandchildren, but also great grandchildren. 'I have 14 grandchildren and five great grandchildren. Quite a family! Rachel was over the moon because it was something she had always wanted. Suddenly she went from being this only child to having a huge family. She had known about them all along though, from when she was quite young I told her about her brother and sisters in Northern Ireland.'

The first reunion took place at the end of January when two of Anne's daughters came to see her in London. It was strange meeting these grown women she had last seen as children. 'But nothing had really changed. Yes, they were older, but still as I had pictured them. I always carried a photo of them with me, that was the only memento I had but, of course, they had grown up!'

The family set about trying to catch up on all the missing lifetimes. 'You'll never be able to catch up really but through the years I always thought about them and wondered about them. I even went to fortune tellers who told me yes, there would be a reunion someday.'

Anne's family are loving and kind. They weren't angry she had left them and the older ones could certainly remember the trauma they all suffered before their mother had been forced to leave. 'There were a lot of things that they could remember and a lot of things they couldn't, so we decided the only way to handle it was that whatever they asked, whatever they wanted to know, I would answer it if I possibly could, whether it was what they wanted to hear or not.'

And what kind of things did they want to ask?

'Well, they didn't really want to know that much because they would have remembered a lot that happened between their daddy and me. But some of them couldn't remember what ages they were when I left. You know I always thought about them and Dan and I used to talk about them a lot but I used to get very upset, so we stopped it, he used to get upset as well. Dan had never met any of them and we just had their childhood photos to remember them.'

But Rachel was quite a surprise to most of her siblings. Anne had told her eldest daughter, Paula, when Rachel was born and had assumed she had told the others but the others were young and didn't really remember the news.

Anne's four children from Northern Ireland had considered their mother missing for more than 20 years. Paula said she always wondered if her mum was alive or dead but another daughter, Emma, said she knew her mother was alive, she just felt it.

So how did the children make contact? 'Emma went on the Internet and got in touch with the Salvation Army. They couldn't trace me but they sent a letter with my former name on it to the National Insurance people in the UK asking if I had an insurance number, and if I had, and an address was available, would they please forward the letter. They sent a covering letter to me saying they had nothing to do with the enclosed letter but were simply asked to forward it.'

The children told Anne they felt they couldn't look for her until their father had died and so it was his death in 2000 that spurred the search. 'They felt guilty about it and they didn't want to upset their daddy either, which I can understand.'

Anne has now been back to Northern Ireland twice to visit her children and their families. 'You can't describe it, it's just wonderful', she says. She likes all her new in-laws and the grandchildren and the great grandchildren. And what do they make of having a granny at long last? 'Some of them knew about me but one of them thought I was dead!'

For now, there are the celebrations, not to mention all those birthdays! 'There's a lot of birthdays', Anne says, 'I think May is the only month when I have no birthdays!'

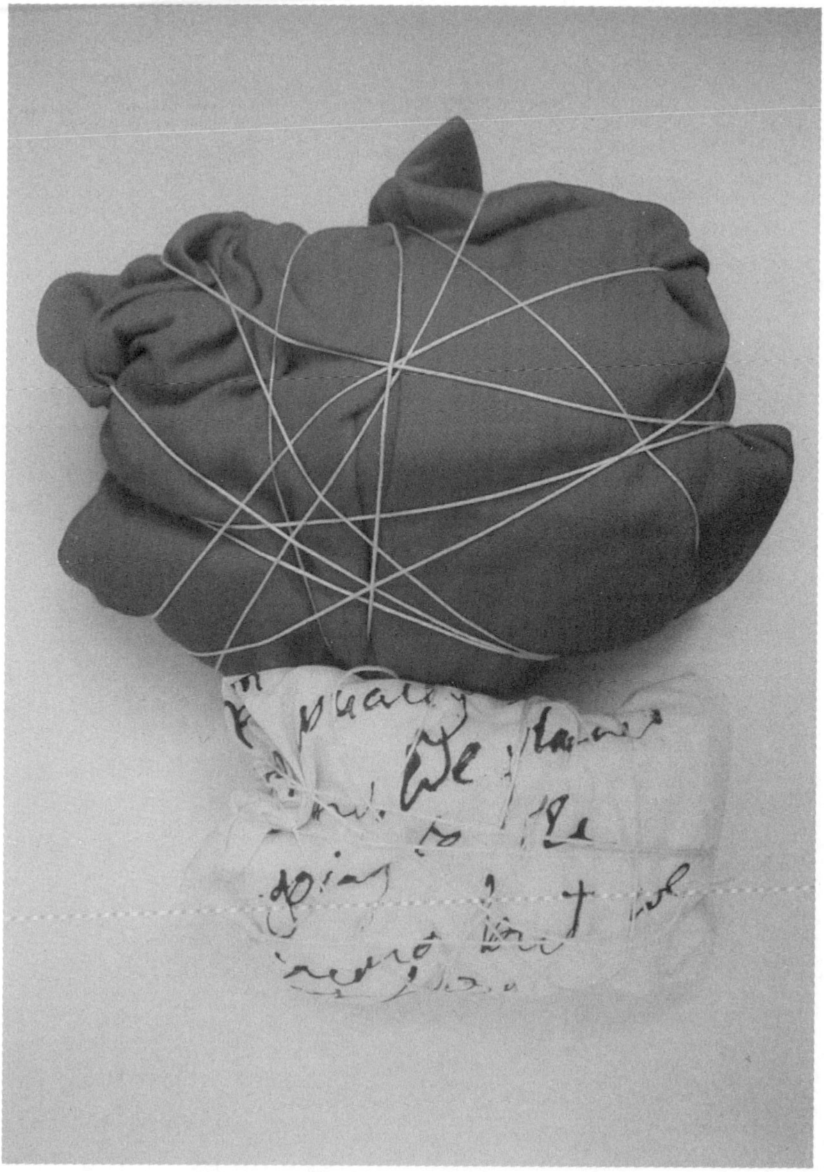

35

Frances Tyrrell

Absent and Present

All 52 faces stare out at you. The longer they are missing, the more faded their picture. It's all in black and white, a mathematical structure, but this puzzle has no solution. These are Ireland's missing people.

In a separate room, photographs of personal objects are bound in twine, wrapped and then placed inside lockers. The objects, unsuccessfully unwrapped, represent 'no closure'.

Frances Tyrrell's exhibition represents the paradox of the missing person. They are 'gone but not gone' at the same time. They are forever locked in a limbo from which they will never break free unless they lose their missing status, unless they are found.

The 22-year-old artist knows the face of every person who went missing in Ireland over the past 30 years. She has devoted a year to completing the exhibition.

The message she aimed to get across was: 'This could be your sister.'

The exhibition was held at Crawford College of Art and Design in Cork City where Frances studied for her degree. The idea was initially born out of the theme Frances had been pursuing in her first and second years: 'Absent and Present'.

Frances cannot recall the exact point at which she decided to create an exhibition of missing people for her final-year art project as she was always very aware of the issue. Her own mother's stepbrother has been missing for the past 20 years and the subject often came up in conversation. She remembers all the coverage in the press about Jo Jo Dullard and Annie McCarrick and could imagine the devastation of the families. All of these issues played a role in Frances creating the exhibition.

She was particularly struck by the number of girls who have gone missing in Ireland over the past 10 years. She was affected by the fact that the girls were all of a similar age to her, and she found herself frequently thinking about it. As the thoughts continued and she was repeatedly reminded of the fact that a huge number of people had disappeared without trace by the various features in the media, she began to think about the possibility of expressing the subject through art.

Coming from Tipperary, Frances lived just down the road from Callan where Jo Jo Dullard went missing. The proximity to the area had a subconscious effect in reminding Frances of Jo Jo's case.

In the summer of 2002, Frances began to research the issue. She surfed the Internet, looking for Missing Persons websites and articles about individuals who had gone missing. The more Frances read, the more fascinated she became with the fact that there were people out there who had just disappeared and, despite in-depth searches, could not be found, dead or alive. Frances began to imagine what it must be like for the families of these people, who had to continue on with their lives not knowing what had happened to their loved one. She watched endless documentaries and read page after page of relevant websites to gather enough information to compile an exhibition. She became more and more drawn into the astounding stories of how one day a person was going about their daily routine, and the next they were not there, a year or years later still 'gone'.

Frances decided on a photographic exhibition which would represent the face of every one of Ireland's missing people. Not wanting to upset families, she took only the photos that were already published on the Missing Persons website. She took the photos and screen-printed them in a lifelike size, 15 × 15 inches. She used just the portraits of the people and put all 52 pictures in a mathematical structure. The pictures were placed in order along a bar graph. There was a time line, the people most recently missing came first, followed by those who went missing before them and gradually going back to the person missing the longest. The ink is stronger in the black and white pictures of those most recently missing, and fades slowly with the fading of the years, as the photographic structure reaches back to those missing the longest.

These are ordinary black and white pictures, Frances has not edited them in any way. She wants to represent the ordinary nature of people who go missing, because she says they are ordinary. 'They could be a friend of yours, someone you know, even a member of your family. I want people to look at this exhibition and think, "This could be my sister".'

The more she worked on the exhibition and the more familiar she became with the individuals, the more Frances began to see likenesses between the missing people and people she knew herself. 'I began to associate them with people I knew, in terms of height and looks and I really wanted to get this angle across so that people could associate their own family and friends with them.'

The reasoning behind this is so that people don't just presume things about those that are missing. She wants to get the message across that there is nothing strange about the individuals who go missing. Her research has revealed to her that they are as ordinary as the next person, however people who don't know about the issue automatically jump to conclusions. 'People hear of a missing person and think "Oh they committed suicide". Most of the time this is not the case.'

Frances used the second room of her exhibition to particularly emphasise the ordinary nature of the people who have gone missing. The objects photographed and locked in the lockers are objects that one would find on any dressing table or any locker. They are ordinary, personal items. Another interesting piece of research in providing a background to the assumptions people make, were the surveys she read through, asking the public to say where they thought missing people had got to. The majority of people guessed at either foul play or suicide.

The reality is that it is never that simple. The status of 'missing' indicates that no body has been found and nobody actually knows where the person is. The cases are shrouded in mystery and you cannot judge without knowing the person. Quite frequently those who go missing are the most normal of individuals, with happy dispositions, plenty of friends and who are very close to their families. That is why their disappearance is so bewildering. Family members believed they knew everything about that person and never imagined for a moment that there could be anything bothering them, at least not something they would not have shared with someone they were so close to. Hence the idea 'That could be my sister'.

Frances was reluctant to upset families by asking them questions about their missing loved ones. She felt the research and materials she had were enough to get the message across. Through the course of her work, however, she did come in contact with a couple of relatives of missing people who talked to her and gave her some insight into the way they were feeling. In fact, a couple of people felt the exhibition was very important and Frances was asked to keep in touch with these people.

Frances was overwhelmed by the response to her project, which was on display for three weeks. Hundreds of people came to see the project, which received coverage both locally and nationally. Word of mouth spread and more and more people came to see the exhibition of Ireland's missing people.

Frances was amazed at the number of people who attended the exhibition who knew someone who was missing. She found that everybody seemed to know of somebody who was missing and the reaction she got was very positive. People said to her that her exhibition would draw attention to the issue of missing people, that the display of pictures would stick in people's minds and the press coverage that came out of it would extend that, and thus assist in spreading the message that there were people out there missing, hopefully providing a further push in finding them.

Frances was so taken by the issue of missing people during her research for the project that she wants to continue to pursue the subject. She has no fixed plans as to what form the next project will take, nor does she have any time frame for having it completed. She says she would love to have it completed by the summer of 2004 but is definitely not setting this limit. She wants to do justice to the issue.

Though she tries to distance herself from the emotional trauma of the issue concerning missing people, Frances says inevitably she found herself caught up emotionally in the subject of her project. 'It's very hard to distance yourself. The exhibition has been very powerful and meaningful to me.' At times it could be very upsetting when she actually thought about the anguish that the families of these missing people must be experiencing.

Any role that the exhibition may have in helping to find missing people is very important. While the project itself may not be responsible for finding anyone, Frances feels there is a spin-off effect brought about through media coverage and word of mouth. She feels her aunt hit the nail on the head as to the potential of the exhibition in locating missing people when she came to see it along with Frances' parents. 'My aunt remembered a programme that was on *Five Seven Live* on RTÉ Radio 1 a couple of months ago, in which they interviewed people whose relatives were missing. Sometimes hearing a programme like this can put a thought into someone's head, they may spread the thought by talking about it and that could provoke someone to do something else. It sets the ball rolling and I feel that that's the way it works with my exhibition. The coverage it gets in the press might get someone thinking about the issue and the word can spread.'

Frances has put huge work into completing her exhibition. She worked on it every day over the course of a year. She now wants to further that work, and though she isn't actively contacting families to interview, she has already spoken to some people whom she met through the course of her work. This was a very particular exhibition. It was not about selling work, rather about expressing something that had a profound effect on her. Since the exhibition, she has received a huge number of letters from people who attended, saying it had a powerful effect on them, either because they were personally connected with someone who was missing or simply because the subject spoke to them in some way, highlighting a very real issue that a lot of people are not really aware of at all.

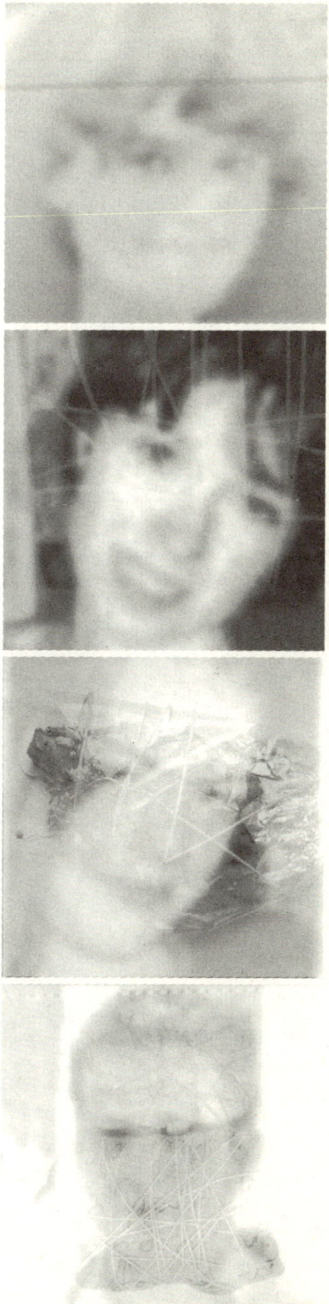

Photos from Frances Tyrrell's exhibition

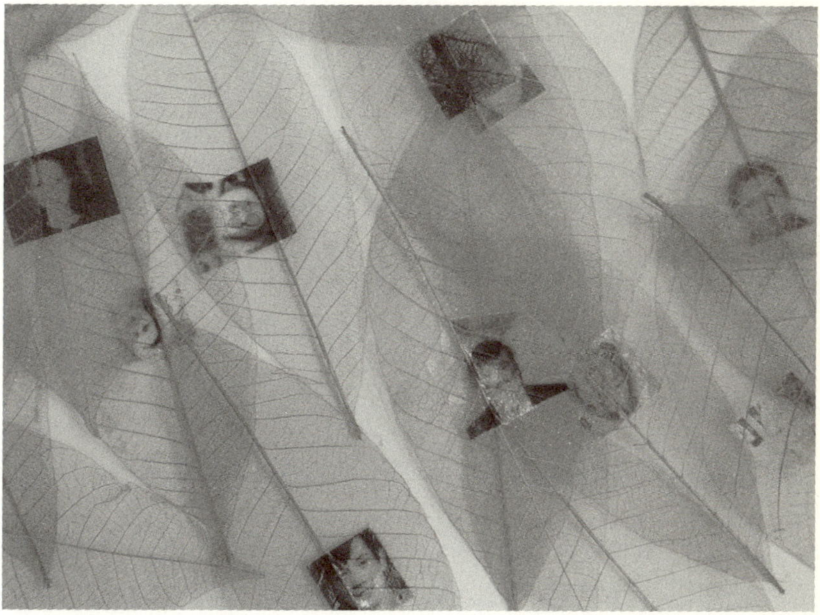

Aztec Prayer to Tezcatlipoca - God of the Sky

Only for so short a while have you loaned us to each other
because we take form in your act of drawing us
as we breathe in your singing to us

but only for a short while
have you loaned us to each other

because even a drawing cut in
crystalline obsidian fades

and the green feathers, the crown feathers
of the quetzal bird lose their colour

and even the sounds of the waterfall
die out in the dry season

so we too because only for a short while
have you loaned us to each other...